The Mystical Life Experiences of The Awakening Shaman

The Mystical Life Experiences of The Awakening Shaman

Linda Ledbeter

Printed in the United States of America

ISBN: 978-1-949513-53-0

Published by Linda Ledbeter

Dedication

The endless list of people, animals and nature who have contributed to my awakening, for as long or short of time we shared space together.

To all the people, animals, and nature your teachings and blessings are imprinted in my heart.

Acknowledgments

Gary, Josh, and Phil, and all the grandchildren who have contributed to my awakening whether as cheerleaders or bystanders.

To the Shamans who played an important role, divinely appearing on the Red Road when needed: Keith Varnum, Dan Huber, Deborah Murphy, Carole Daly, Carol Michalski, Rainbow Eagle, and Kristiana Bloom.

To my friends and family: Marilyn Bignell, we may have been born sisters living separate lives for my first eighteen years, but we are indeed bookends. My Rev. Sisters—Ellen Laperriere, Pam McDonal, Iris Kuehl, Annie Horzen, Sherryl Andrus—we created change in our lives and in the lives of others. Lois Reetz, Pam Kackelmeier, Joel Gollhart, James Patt, Lisa Young, Jim and Cindi Schickert, Cory Corrigan, and so many more people walked with me as I sometimes crawled and ran through life, blessing and forgiving each other. Sherry Mikkleson, special thank you for your gift of the poem.

A special appreciation to the editors with The DP Group, LLC. Divya Parekh has been a constant fountain of wisdom, knowledge, and support.

To all the animals that have taught and loved each other as family. The fifty-plus foster dogs over the course of thirty years touched my heart with their courage and strength to trust when asked to do so. The first authentic smile, the first full trusting tail swish, the confident walks, and let's not forget your confident walk with your new forever family, remain imprinted in my heart. For those who were so broken that living a healthy, happy life wasn't in the picture, your passing in my arms was my gift to you.

To our small piece of land that became my sanctuary: thank you for your beauty and grounding.

Table of Contents

Foreword

There are times in life when the path ahead isn't clearly marked yet somehow reveals itself through the magnetic pull of the land, a whisper from the unknown, or the quiet companionship of animals guiding our steps. *The Mystical Life Experiences of the Awakening Shaman* is a living testament to what unfolds when we choose to trust instinct, spirit, and the unseen world.

Linda Ledbeter invites us to walk beside her as she follows these mystical experiences —the subtle clues, and chance encounters, that have drawn her deeper into the heart of the shamanic path. Her journeys carry us through the Ocooch High Hills, across ancient stone ledges, into red rock mountains, and through the challenges of family struggles. Each step is woven with ancestral memory, moments of separation, and descents into the subconscious realms of healing and transformation.

This is not a book of abstract concepts or distant theories. It is rooted in lived experiences: the fatigue of a body in pain, the awe of unexpected blessings, the vulnerability of standing before the unknown.

Linda's stories do not instruct you on how to awaken the shaman within. Instead, she offers an initiation of a lived glimpse of what it means to walk with spirit, to embody mystery, and to live guided by unseen hands. If you open to these pages, they may awaken a deep memory or the call of the shaman that has always been within you, waiting to emerge.

Pam Kackelmeier

Reviews

Linda Ledbeter narrates her life journey with a focus on her inner spiritual life, grappling with profound universal questions and powerful, personal transformative experiences. She highlights practical advice, personal transformation, and fresh insights, and she explores the process of questioning and discovery itself. She advocates being realistic and straightforward, encouraging readers to embrace timeless lessons and take action in their lives. The author focuses on transformation and practicality. This book does a skillful job of mixing deep spiritual ideas with a pragmatic perspective, helping readers find inner freedom and understand themselves better.

Ledbeter writes in a way that's honest, direct, easy to understand, and very impactful, revealing options on how to deal with the ups and downs of your mind and feelings. She provides clear examples of stepping back from mental chatter and letting go of hindering thoughts, making her tale a toolkit for emotional and spiritual liberation. If applied, the insights in this book will not only change your inner life, but also cause an inner awakening to be birthed within you.

The book's themes explore the tension between actively seeking spiritual truth and surrendering to a divine plan or higher power. The author expresses her experiences of feeling lost or restless, leading her to embark on a conscious search for purpose, fulfillment, and a quest for meaning. These memoirs often depict a critical moment where the author must let go of her own control, intellect, or expectations and surrender to a higher will, a spiritual tradition, or an inner knowing. With moving stories involving humans and animals, she explores grief, loss, and healing. She confronts tragedy and death as catalysts for profound spiritual insights.

Her themes examine how individuals can find light in darkness, and hope and spiritual meaning in the face of despair. Far from being a sign of weakness, doubt is a central theme, where questioning one's beliefs becomes a path to a more authentic faith. The spiritual journey then becomes one of rebuilding a more personal, nuanced, and authentic set of beliefs. She recounts the difficult process of letting go of grudges and resentment, a choice that frees her from internal bondage. The journey toward forgiveness, both of others and of oneself, is a powerful redemptive theme. A major focus in her stories is the experience of undeserved grace, which allows the author to forgive herself for past mistakes and find redemption, revealing a powerful testament to the healing and transformative power of forgiveness.

Her first-person narration allows for a direct, intimate, and often vulnerable connection between the author and reader. It creates a sense of immediacy and fosters empathy as the reader experiences the author's journey firsthand. She makes effective use of highly specific, sensory-vivid details to recall past spiritual epiphanies or moments of crisis. This approach creates a more powerful and immediate experience for the reader. She blends a subjective account of events with a more objective, retrospective analysis. The author looks back at her younger self or a past experience and reinterprets it through the lens of her current spiritual understanding.

She skillfully uses metaphor and simile. These devices are crucial for describing intangible spiritual concepts in tangible, relatable terms. She employs symbolism well to represent universal spiritual truths. She uses allegory masterfully by telling a story where characters, settings, or events are used to represent abstract spiritual concepts. I applaud her choice of presenting her life adventures as stand-alone stories.

Keith Varnum

Author Linda Ledbeter's latest offering, *The Mystical Life Experiences of the Awakening Shaman*, takes readers on a deeper dive into her daunting journey of survival, including her unconventional path to spiritual arrival.

Besides touching on her abusive, formative years in a very dysfunctional family, the book describes a series of experiences where she discovers her gift and ability to communicate with animals. Ledbeter shares valuable examples of how learning to communicate with a dog, for example, is a lot like learning to effectively communicate with a kid or an adult.

The path of becoming an "animal whisperer" also drove her to a deeper understanding of the spiritual world, opening up new understandings and beliefs, including going "kicking and screaming" into the world of Shamanism. The reader tags along, entrenched in her journey, as she describes how learning to trust herself was the key to her "awakening to spirituality."

On the lighter side, at one point she decides it's important to tackle her fear of snakes with an attempt to communicate with them. Her experience exemplifies why we need to be careful and intentional in what we wish for!

Dennis Warner, Singer and Songwriter

Socrates

The unexamined life is not worth living!

Introduction

The Mystical Experiences of the Awakening Shaman is a trail of experience guided by past and present events, leading the reluctant and yet curious me into shaking off the shadows that kept me silent. I didn't always understand the why or the what of it. Intuitively, I knew it was important. As I gathered and examined my thoughts and beliefs, I unleashed something primal; deep inside, a lioness slept, waiting for her chance to escape. She did and never looked back.

In a journey, the Elder and I sat around a fire under the night sky in the Upper World shared that the book *Mirror Mirror on All Fours* had passed. Begin writing your mystical experiences. No reason given, just write. Shifting my awareness from a meditative state back into my room, the stack of books on my desk from Deb and several others I had gravitated to gave me insight into the first clue. To date, nothing I have read resembled my experiences. Two came close: one was marrying the Bible with shamanism, the other, being accepted into the beehive. Are there others like me who have had mystical experiences that led them deeper into their awakening?

I live an ordinary and extraordinary life all rolled into one. In my youth, I was naïve and certainly not ready for the real world. While writing my memoir *Sacred Life, Sacred Death*, the realization that my mother and foster family willfully kept me ignorant struck a chord. The reason my mother gave was to keep me from stepping into the "pitfalls" of life. The foster home did so to protect themselves—sheltering versus preparing me for life. With their need to protect me, I became prey for conspiracy theories. What I needed to be sheltered from was granted to me by the courts.

In my early adulthood, I began to recognize the connective behaviors between the animals and myself. Anxiety and abandonment were the breeding grounds for my lack of confidence, hidden in an armor of self-assurance, a "fake it 'til you make it" attitude. That attitude didn't feel authentic. Faking was still faking. Smiling and laughing were natural for me, as were anger and despair.

My first face-off with possible death in my early twenties was a pivotal moment. The bleeding ulcers' message was simple: "It's not what you are eating, it's what's eating you." I had several emotional breakdowns as an adult, including depression from the burning subterranean anger. In my late fifties, I screamed into the room, telling

Jesus that if He really existed, He had better show up because I couldn't stand how angry I felt. The fear of the anger's depth and grip was like a volcano slowly erupting. He manifested before my eyes, and we had what some would call the "Come to Jesus Moment." In all my studies and adventures, Jesus walked beside me, even when I didn't know it. Together we have healed others of cancer, done spiritual surgery, assisted in reducing pain from surgeries and injuries, and guided others to ask, seek, and receive.

It took me decades to acknowledge that I was practicing shamanism. Impostor syndrome walked beside me, even with evidential proof. Jesus is a shaman! In John 14:12, He speaks clearly that those who believe can and will do the same work, and even greater. Shamans lived in all cultures long before Jesus's birth and still walk among us.

My guides, angels, and teachers had their work cut out for them when I entered this plane of existence. As my grandfather so kindly said to me in a recent journey, my sister and I came in like a wrecking ball.

As I wrote, new insights and clarity began to rise from the ashes like the phoenix rising. Just when I thought the book was complete, I realized there were two chapters missing during my journaling. The thoughts and emotions centered around the changes within myself were now far-reaching within the family dynamics and were dancing around in my head, sounding like five bands playing simultaneously in a crowded ballroom. Journaling quieted the bands, and a new song emerged. The "why" for sharing my life experiences had emerged as I wrote.

If you are a Seeker of Truth, then travel with me in the uprising of our souls, finding our voices and standing our ground in peace. Allow the messages within these pages to inspire and encourage you to choose to free your authentic self, no matter how crazy it may seem or how broken you think you are.

Dare to dance your dance, sail your vessel, and live your life in freedom.

Chapter 1
Tiny's Wiggling Demise

It is hard to fathom a child under three years of age remembering with clarity and understanding the significance of the events unfolding in their lives. I was an oddity; the black sheep, some would say. Learning to find the flow within the ever-shifting, unstable family unit as the youngest child was achieved by observation. While I was imprinting events and their significance into my memory banks, others were washing and sweeping the unpleasantness into the shadows. Piece by piece, aspects of their souls left the body to survive.

Hearing and watching the anger and hatred between our parents and the disdain Father directed at our mother permeated the air. I remember Tiny wiggling in my two-year-old arms as if it were yesterday.

Tiny was Mother's Chihuahua. She enjoyed dogs that she could place in her apron pocket. Tiny was a perfect fit. He was small, weighing in at about three pounds. His coat was light copper brown in color, with big brown bug eyes and ears larger than his head. Tiny was a youngster, around a year old, full of wiggles and attitude.

We lived on a rented farm, nestled in a green valley surrounded by hills brimming with healthy hardwood trees. The two-story farmhouse was in desperate need of a fresh coat of white paint. The clapboard siding, steps, and porch floors were once white but now a weathered gray with chipped lead paint. Bare wood was exposed to the natural elements of sun, rain, snow, and human traffic. From the front yard, the red barn sat to the left of the house, with a large corral for the workhorses. The driveway bore a path separating the yard from the corral.

On this particular day, the sky was blue with white, fluffy clouds. A summer breeze blew my soft, fine blonde hair about my face. Dad's siblings and their spouses had come to tend to the foal in the barn. Mom, my sisters, brother, and I stood next to the white wooden fence, anticipating the frolicking foal as it was released into the corral.

I loved the horses with their strong, muscular bodies, the proud arch of their necks and heads, the graceful dancing gait moving in rhythm to the music deep within their soul. Their brown eyes bore into my heart with equal force as did their mere presence. I was unaware of what the draw meant, only that it ran deep and wild, combined with a gentle soothing that ignited a fire in my heart.

Today was no different. I watched between the wooden fence planks in anticipation of the foal's grand appearance. There he was, in all his splendor with a golden brown coat, white socks, and a blaze of white down his face. Encouragement wasn't needed for him to take off in a full run within the corral's perimeter. He held his long, graceful legs, head, and tail high with pride. His soft knickers of gratitude and appreciation filled the air.

Standing next to Mom, securely cradling Tiny in her arms, my relentless pleading to hold him led her to place him in my tiny arms with a promise to hold him tightly. Once in my arms, he wanted down. Tiny began wiggling and twisting for freedom; my two-year-old arms were unable to control his twisting little body. In an instant, he was running full speed into the corral, chasing and barking behind the foal.

I watched the unfolding in slow motion, adults screaming for Tiny to stop. The shouting voices, coupled with Tiny's nipping and barking at the foal's feet, filled the air. Terror filled his eyes, and his joyful dance turned into panic. The sound of the foal's hoof making contact with his small head, followed by a sharp yelp, filled the air, and then, deafening silence. Tiny lay motionless while the foal ran in nervous circles.

Dad ran to where he had fallen in the dust, scooping up his lifeless body, Mom screaming beside me that he was only knocked out. The foal's frantic gallop slowed to an anxious trot as his eyes filled with terror even after the danger had passed.

Mom carried his lifeless body up to the side of the hill for burial, followed by her children. Under the layer of the grass-covered hillside, ancient rock and sediments untouched from the glaciers supported the roots of the majestic trees that sang their own mourning song with the summer breeze. Digging his grave for such a small body was difficult, yet she managed.

Kneeling next to the grave, my hands tucked under my legs, I recall observing my family's reactions. Mother's grieving sobs, coupled with the litany of blaming Dad and his family, penetrated the air. Dad's history of indifference turned her grief into full-blown anger and resentment.

My two sisters, kneeling on the ground across from his resting place, remained silent and unmoving. Were they paying attention to her angry protests against the carelessness of the adults? Did they even care about Tiny? Maybe they had learned to tune everything out, becoming numb?

Mom's crushing sobs and anger pointed directly at Dad and his family, and not toward me, was the first pivotal moment in my life. Why wasn't I blamed? It was I who lost control of his wiggling body. I wondered why she blamed others who had nothing to do with the situation, except for tending to the foal. They were, after all, on the other side of the corral.

I wondered why she saw herself as blameless. Didn't she know I was too small to hold onto a puppy under these conditions? Or did she?

Under calmer conditions in the past, I had held him comfortably. How long could a two-year-old's arms hold a wiggling, determined puppy? Why didn't she say no, or maybe she didn't know how to say "no" to anyone?

Looking upon Mom's grief-stricken face and tear-filled eyes, and then to those of my siblings with their dry and distant gazes, I instinctively recognized the emotional distancing of themselves from the harsh realities of living. Tears streaked down my small face for the loss of Tiny, for the sadness I saw in those around me, and for my part in his death.

This was the first of several memories prior to my fourth birthday. I had successfully convinced her to let me traipse into the woods where, earlier in the week, my siblings and I had played. They were at school, and I was bored. Confidently, I walked into the woods, believing that I knew the way; I didn't.

Alone and scared, I turned around, looking for something familiar. There were trees that touched the sky far above my head, sounds of the late summer breeze swishing the leaves, and sun streaming down in the small open, unfamiliar meadow. Hair stood up on the back of my neck, and it felt like something was watching my movements.

Turning around, I saw and heard nothing to validate my senses. I turned and ran, hoping that if I could run fast enough, my feet would take me in the direction of home. Before exiting the woods into our yard, I slowed my pace to a walk, showing fear and having to admit I didn't know the way would make me weak.

A few days later, a rabid coyote was shot in the neighbor's barn a few hundred feet from where I had stood lost in the woods.

Just as I was questioning the events around Tiny's death, I wondered why my mother would allow me to go unattended into the woods. The Mississippi Driftless Area was alive with predatory animals; more than one hunter had gotten lost during deer season. What power did I hold over her that I could talk her into anything, or maybe she just didn't care anymore?

Strange that I didn't consider the possibility that I wasn't important to her. Because I was questioning and analyzing the people and events, it didn't occur to me that others were not. My angels and guides walked beside me and communicated the answers in a way I understood.

Chapter 2
The Notorious Haunted House on the Corner

Mother had managed to divorce Father after several unsuccessful attempts. I was around three years old when she attempted to leave the first time. Father was in the field with my older brother when she hustled us into the car, barefoot and dirty. There wasn't time for shoes as we had to go. Without resources for a mother and children, we were back a few days later.

Mom kept me shielded from the physical beatings she endured while strapped naked to the clothesline pole by Dad and his family. Her offense was suspicion of adultery. The two older sisters had to have known. I have questioned whether my older brother was present during the beatings. Shortly after, she disappeared. We were told that she was sick and mentally weak.

My baby brother arrived. Dad was thrilled to have a boy to carry on the family name. The girl children had to be her failure or someone else's.

After her successful divorce, she struggled to keep us fed and clothed and was forced to move to the nearest larger town to find employment. The eldest sister, thirteen years older than me, had been living elsewhere before I was two years old. Our brother stayed with Dad after he ran away from us several times.

Four of us packed our meager belongings and moved into a small house just inside the city limits for the next few years. During that time, the eldest of the four disappeared from my life. No explanations except that she was sick and getting help. Then there were three.

Mother had met a man and decided to move closer to work as a caregiver for his aging mother and as a housekeeper and cook for him. She rented a house, packed us up without explanation, and drove us to our new home. Turning into the driveway, the windows appeared black. The two-story house felt like it rose up directly from the ground. What was once a yard was transformed into a sea of grass nearly as tall as me. I was almost seven years old and terrified of the unknown feelings of fear.

Walking through the towering sea of grass, making my way to the door, my stomach knotted, throat constricted, fear trickled down my neck. These new sensations of fear heightened when I first stepped onto the neglected wooden steps. Now I felt my heart race, blood rushing to my head, clouding my vision and hearing. There was nowhere to run.

On the first level, the walls and windows were covered with soot from the oil burner. Outside, we couldn't see in; when inside, we could see out. The kitchen, even in a child's eyes, was unfit to prepare food. Upstairs, the windows and walls were assaulted by the oil fumes. The three bedrooms and hallway walls were covered in peeling wallpaper. Someone once loved this house.

We were told not to go into the bedroom at the end of the hall. Like any obedient child, I kept my curiosity to investigate in check until weeks later.

It didn't take long for the activity to be noticed by everyone. We heard the sounds of the brittle windowpanes breaking on the second floor daily. The three of us cautiously investigated and found nothing broken. Inaudible voices hung in the air as if in a private conversation. Other times, I knew what was being said. From the corner of my eye, I caught glimpses of movement that disappeared when I looked in that direction. The feeling of never being alone was constant, even when I was the only one in the room.

I began to "see" pig- and monkey-like creatures with wings flying outside the upstairs hall windows. I saw a goat-like creature hanging around me. He told the others that I was his as he caressed my neck with his gnarly fingers.

It was time to investigate the third bedroom. Sucking in air, one step in front of the other, the closed door loomed closer. My shaking hand touched the doorknob. It felt cold in my hand. Dread filled my belly and the hair on my arms and neck stood up. I was going to face my fear. I would not shrink away and do as I was told. Something was living with us, and I wanted to know who or what it was. Another breath in, I tightened my hold on the doorknob and opened the door.

Empty.

The walls, like all the other bedrooms, were covered in peeling wallpaper. This room had red and pink flowered paper and was the largest bedroom. Something unpleasant happened in that room. Is that why we were told to stay away?

We spent close to a year with many abnormal activities in and outside that are beyond a typical haunting. The house was burned down, hoping to stop the activity. Everyone who stepped on the property felt its existence. The house may be gone but the activity remains.

To this day, nobody is allowed to touch my neck. I have lived in several haunted houses, and there is a difference in my mind between a haunting and visitations. Over the years, I have learned and unlearned and then learned again the different beliefs regarding hauntings, the different levels of dark energies, entities, demonic forces, curses, and so much more. We have studied and trusted our guides and, for me, Jesus, how to discern the method and approach for a successful clearing.

It has been taught within the multitude of religions and ideologies that only Light exists and therefore all else doesn't exist. I will say, within my experiences, when I practiced denying anything other than Light existed, I was proven wrong. Not everyone can or should take these situations on. There is a time and place to engage or not to engage. Leave it to those who have been called to do so.

Chapter 3

Good Intentions Are Not Enough

The fifteen-pound, soft, furry, multi-colored, one floppy ear, soft deep, brown-eyed puppy, touched with a sparkle of mischief, was our undoing. Sargent was our first dog as new parents; our son was two years old at the time. We agreed he should have a dog, just as we did growing up.

Oftentimes, puppies removed from their littermates and mom may have some anxiety issues. I didn't know this, among other important information. Unbeknownst to us, we had become his new pack. Our ignorance was that he was only a dog like all the other farm dogs. Wrong. Farm dogs and family dogs have different rules and expectations. Pets need to learn how to live with people. It's not the dog's fault; rather, it's the well-intentioned parent, and we know how far good intentions will get you when your skill level is zero.

Returning home from my daily walk with our son, we were greeted with my sewing patterns shredded like confetti on the floor. The following day, I tied the dog to the table leg with a bone to keep him comfortable. The next day, I tied him outside. He barked the whole time. Even after a week, the barking didn't cease. A three-month-old, fifteen-pound pup wasn't being naughty but afraid to be alone. He wasn't being naughty when he didn't come when called; my husband had made it a game, just like the farm dogs. Like all young parents, we didn't know what we didn't know about raising children and pets. I was expecting a lot without the knowledge to back it up.

Casper, the white male kitten, and Sargent became best of friends. Again, I, the naïve and clueless young adult, still believed that cats and dogs were natural-born enemies. I took literally the phrase "fight like cats and dogs." The farm cats and dogs always got along, so why did this phrase sit as truth?

Casper was loyal as a dog is loyal. During the moving phase, when we bought our first house, I thought it was safer for him to remain in the only home he knew during the move. Returning for the last load, Casper was displaying anxiety, panting and fearfully crying loudly.

My own emotions of abandonment had risen to the surface yet again. The first time I felt this guilt, I hadn't learned from it. Sargent was left home alone while we trekked off on a three-day Christmas trip. He had gone with us many times; this time there wasn't room for him. The neighbor had agreed to check in on him during our absence.

We returned home to an empty house. He had escaped and followed our scent before he was picked up thirty miles away by the police. My heart sank. Guilt stabbed like a knife, penetrating the heart that meant no harm. How could I have not known what it was like for them?

I saw myself separate from the animals. I had been taught that animals don't have the emotions and the mental processes of the superior human, as the Bible states.

Good intentions don't excuse not taking responsibility to dig deeper into my why. The why and the what questions, I learned later, are called "shadow work." My excuses were symptoms of a deeper, psychologically knotted belief system that kept me in control and animals separate. How could I love animals and still not see the depth of their love and devotion until I had caused unnecessary harm?

The unlearning had begun, making room for the awakening. I had inspiring intentions to be a good pet owner. My driving force was not to make the same mistakes as well-meaning adults in my life had made. The mirrored connection between the results of my actions with my pets had begun. I had years of self-evaluation ahead of me.

The paved road of good intentions is rocky at best. We don't know what we don't know. Take time for self-evaluation to determine what is yours to claim and what isn't. Let the awakening begin.

Chapter 4
The Magic of a Dog's Heart

We had moved from southwestern Wisconsin across the state to eastern Wisconsin, close to Lake Michigan. A few years later, we moved again. This time an hour plus north where we eventually purchased property and established a home.

For three years, living in a townhouse surrounded by unscrupulous people with ceaseless revving engines, squealing tires, horns honking at the car in front, neighbors screaming, and the conversations that could be heard through the dividing wall. It all blocked out the natural songs of nature. The church we had joined, and that eventually hired me to lead the youth group, turned from a joyful position to hostility. The expectation that I was to "fix" a problem I supposedly was responsible for within two months was impossible. It was created by my superior and a volunteer leader. I resigned.

The leaders of the church didn't send me off with an explanation to the congregants. Thus, it was assumed I was guilty of a crime. Those who once saw me as a leader now looked through me, past me, and over my head. I had become a living ghost. Depression had taken over, faith had failed me, joy had been replaced by an empty spiritual void.

Anticipation didn't sweep the void into nonexistence; it had given me something to wake up to. The closest neighbor was four acres away, surrounded by woods. Life in the city had sucked my soul empty. The wildlife and the land held me up, even when I was unaware most days. The future yard needed to be groomed for planting grass, possible flower gardens staked out, and a vegetable garden. All of us worked together.

The boys, now young teenagers, were promised they could have a pet of their choosing. Teka, the Siberian husky pup, was one of the choices. I loved the breed for its resemblance to a wolf. Independence and their free-spirited energy were untameable. She knew who was in charge, and it wasn't us. We were her bonded pack, at her convenience. Every fence was her challenge. Whatever I thought I had learned over the years, she proved me wrong.

Teka arrived and passed during my awakening phase from naivety. I was expecting her to be compliant, which went against her strong alpha energy. It was who she was! She was mirroring back to me a reflection of myself. Others saw me as a free spirit and a wise leader, which was the complete opposite of my own viewpoint.

With her only litter of puppies, we watched her nurture them with grace and innate wisdom, unlike humans. As each one was born, she cleaned them up, then nudged me to pick each one up, greeting them into our world. After two days of not leaving her family's side, we gently took her by the collar and walked her outside.

It was late spring. The five-week-old puppies, full of life, were chasing their mother around the last of the snow and taking over every inch of the house. Teka mourned as five of the six left for their new life. After her spay, she mourned the passing of another litter. She visited where she gave birth, where she and her babies made their beds in the house, along with their late-spring kennel outside. It took a week before she settled into a new norm. A single female pup with blue eyes, named Angel, remained with us.

I was working twelve- to fourteen-hour days running a cleaning business while helping a single sick mother with her three small children. Nearly at my breaking point, I told my husband to get me out of here for a few days. As I was rushing out the door, I stopped, looking back at four sets of worried faces staring up at me: Teka, Angel, and the two cats, Spencer and Sassy.

Gathering what little sanity I had left, I looked Teka in the eyes, saying, "I'm sorry I have been horrible lately. I have to get away to breathe. I'm asking you to let the others know that we will return in a few days, and Jodie will be here to take care of you."

Before returning home as promised, I connected with Teka in the spirit realm, letting her know I was better and coming home. Opening the door, Angel, Sassy, and Spencer sat side by side, Teka sitting behind them. The four sets of eyes looked up at me and remained sitting in place. Dropping to my knees, I hugged each one before taking Teka in my lap, hugging and crying with gratitude. As much as she challenged me, her love ran deep and pure.

After Teka's passing from cancer, Angel and I walked the Kettle Moraine trails several times a week. She was the opposite of her mother. She was a follower with a huge heart. Huskies are known for their escape artistry from any fence and recall can be questionable, but their love is endless.

Angel Blue was different. If I couldn't hear or see her, I called out, "Angel, I can't see you," and within seconds, her head peeked out of the bushes. She was one of two dogs I trusted to walk off leash on the trails.

The willingness to see myself through their eyes and take responsibility was not always an easy task. Facing my shadow side, I was actually meeting myself for the first time. I was developing emotional maturity and taking ownership of my undeveloped innate skills. The world changed when my attitude changed.

As the years passed with my studies, putting into practice what I was learning, and most importantly, listening to my intuition, I became known as the animal whisperer. In the span of twenty years, we have fostered over sixty displaced dogs, most suffering from mild to severe trauma. My success rate for their recovery and adoptions was remarkable. A handful could not be saved for various reasons, and they rest peacefully on our property. These dogs also showed me they are not afraid to die. Acceptance of death is part of living. Giving birth is sacred, and so is holding them as they pass over into spirit form.

By taking the time to learn who they are, what their needs are to live joyfully, and to be seen as having intelligence and feelings is only the beginning. Animals, like us, display unhealthy behaviors when we are not seen, heard, or respected. They are given no choices, only expectations.

When they arrive here, especially those with depression or who have lost hope, I have a heart to heart sit-down discussion with them giving them a choice to allow me to see who they truly are or to receive assistance to leave their body. Every time, within twenty-four hours, trusting me was their choice.

Mirroring back, when children lose hope, they act out, too. They are expected to comply and carry on. Children being moved from foster home to foster home is exactly the same as when rescues keep moving animals around. There is no security, stable structures, or real love. It's only another roof and more unattainable expectations. This leads to dysfunctional adults, and we wonder why the system isn't working. This is the definition of insanity.

Bella, a one-year-old Great Pyrenees, arrived with the worst PTSD and anxiety I and my veterinarian had seen. By thinking outside the box of convention, within a year, she was cured and successfully adopted out.

Lola, a Great Pyrenees and Lab mix, came to us on four different anxiety and pain medications. Within twenty-four hours, she became weak and had difficulty walking with her head down, tongue out, and drooling. While sitting on the floor in the veterinarian room with her, I asked her to give us a chance to get to know who she is, and that she has permission just to be. The following morning, she greeted us with bright eyes and a wagging tail.

Benjamin Riley suffered from depression and severe hot spots, with only a few patches of fur on his body. He was willing himself to die, unresponsive with no hope. Sitting beside his open crate, which he refused to move from in his foster home, I shared with him that we would support his decision to leave his body. We would love to help him find hope and love and to give us a chance. The following morning, he greeted the family, drank, and took food.

Ernie was a case all his own. He lacked impulse control as he was a joy-filled, bouncing bundle of fur, legs, and teeth. Every day for months, we started over with basic training. My legs were covered in bruises from my defensive moves blocking his launching body slams. The handler, Cory, who delivered him to our home, received a cracked jaw when he leaped from a sitting position straight into her face.

It was an early winter evening when he and I were outside for the final run of the day. I was enjoying the snow and the moon shadows of the fifty-acre woods when it crossed my mind to see where Ernie was. Out of the corner of my eye, I glimpsed his forty-five-pound, flowing gold and white furry body midair on a direct line for my knees. I experienced my body being lifted into the air upon impact, slamming onto the frozen ground, head bouncing like a basketball, and my hands still in my coat pockets.

Between my veterinarian and me, Ernie had opened the door to recognizing generational entities. If it were not for this information, Ernie would have been euthanized. Removing the entities was a game changer.

All things are possible when you are willing to believe and seek out the many possibilities. The Healing Touch techniques I had been learning, and the technology my two trusted veterinarians guided me to consider, helped save these beautiful and remarkable beings.

Is this possible for people? I believe it is when they decide they can do their shadow work, learn to forgive, and continue with new resolve. Giving back hope is a game changer.

Chapter 5

Kokopelli Takes My Hand

I was encouraged to attend a retreat guided by a Shaman. My first thought was, *Oh hell no! I'm not getting dragged into satanism!* Yet, there I was attending the retreat anyway. It was a few miles away, and if I felt threatened, I didn't have to return the following day.

Meditation and shamanism were shunned in Western culture as the devil's doorway. I walked through that door with trepidation and curiosity. Keith and Sulana, the shaman leaders, explained in detail what shamanism is and isn't and described the upper world, middle world, and lower world. It seemed sensible and intriguing.

The first journey's intention was to walk down into the underworld. I stalled and stammered, halting midway between the middle world and the lower world, not trusting myself to take another step. The old tape recorder began to play in my mind. Uncertainty's small fingers clutched my heart, warning me not to delve into Satan's domain. Listening to the drum's heartbeat, I called out mentally for help.

A male voice called out to me, *"Linda, you have done this a thousand times before."* A dark, hunched-back figure appeared, playing a flute and sporting spiked hair. Odd that I felt no fear of this strange dude showing up in my journey. Whoever he was, he answered my call for help. Either that, or I have a wild imagination.

Me: "I don't trust. If you want me to keep going, then you are going to meet me halfway. I am not going any further."

He says: "You are learning to trust again. You have done this a thousand times before; you just don't remember."

Me: "Okay, but I'm still not taking another step further down this path."

He says: "Okay, take my hand, and we will stand here together."

Instantly, I found myself stepping out of the tunnel and into a valley. The trees were all dead. I knew intuitively there had been a forest fire or a disease that had swept the land. My attention was then drawn over to my left. A large hill sloped down into the valley below. An eagle appeared in the sky, cresting the ridge of the hill, landing on a dead tree overlooking the dead trees and land.

I was being called back before I could ask what was happening or what it meant. I went back into the tunnel and exited the base of the tree back into the room. Fifteen minutes had passed.

While listening to the participants share their experiences, I sat back, regaining my bearings. After I had described the funky man with the flute and spiked hair, a woman sat up straighter with a shocked and somewhat dumbfounded response, "Kokopelli came to you!?"

"Koco who?"

The facilitator looked at me, and with a slight nod, acknowledged that I was waking up to a whole new world of existence.

That evening, I did some research on this *Koco* person. I was not impressed! Fertility? Chosen one? Oh, I simply don't need or want any more children! This is not happening. I don't believe it. Still, I planned on returning the following morning.

During the REM state prior to waking the following morning, the message came that Kokopelli was a traveler. While he had lain with chosen women of each tribe he visited, he also carried seeds that would be used for growing food. Another metaphor for seeds is spiritual growth, like the mighty mustard seed referred to in the Bible. Have faith.

During our morning share, I explained what I had found and the message received in the morning. A few participants shook their heads, only able to see him as the man who impregnated women as he traveled. Our shaman facilitator didn't take a stance one way or the other but agreed that I was definitely on a new path.

In the afternoon, during another journey with Kokopelli's assistance, I practiced *trust.* Trust that I wasn't falling into satanism or turning away from Christianity. This time, I found myself standing in a meadow of grass. Intuitively, I knew it was on a hill with tall, large pines as their branches with multiple shades of greens and blue swayed in the cool mountain breeze. Clear blue sky was overhead, with the sun's rays shining down upon the land.

In the middle of the yellow grassy meadow sat a young Indian maiden, dressed in a white buckskin dress. A multicolored belt around her waist draped at her side, resting in the grass where she sat. Her black braided hair was styled with a single feather that danced in the summer breeze.

I was in awe of her beauty, although only her back was visible. Radiating off her was contemplation, peace, compassion, gentleness, pride, and the certainty of her position within the tribe. She was a warrior and a leader, holding a prominent position. She was respected and about to be joined with a respected warrior.

Kokopelli appeared everywhere after the weekend retreat. People randomly gave me Kokopelli gifts, even when they didn't understand the significance. They were simply compelled to do so. It was the beginning of a huge shift in my awakening to a new reality.

Chapter 6

The Medium: You Carry a Great Light

A week or two after the retreat, one of my employees had a kidney relapse. She was unable to take care of her three small children. The twins were four years of age and the third almost three, so basically triplets. Kokopelli's appearance indicated children would be entering my life, and here they were, but not as I expected. The retreat participants were right; children were coming my way.

My insistence that fertility was more than human population, and that I didn't need to have more children, remained firm. My children were adults, and I, too, had a life to live outside parenting. Kokopelli's image continued to show up on a regular basis. Maybe his image was everywhere, and I simply hadn't noticed it.

One of the children came grocery shopping with me. Upon leaving, she spotted the children's toy slot machine in the entrance and begged for a dime. She inserted the dime, turned the crank until she heard the sound of surprise fall into the return slot. Her tiny hands opened the plastic capsule. Kokopelli fell out.

The following spring, I was invited to a Medium and Readers event. I had absolutely no idea what it involved, let alone what it was. Being the newbie to all of this, I wanted to walk bravely forward with as much caution as possible. I was dabbling my toes in the water of the unknowing. So far, I hadn't been struck by lightning, only the recurrence of that darn fertility guy, Kokopelli.

Well, if I were to believe the message that the seeds he carried from village to village were for growing food, and that he also carried the seeds to awakening to spirituality, then one step at a time. His message to me was to trust. Trust was difficult, but with the exploring of this new world I had been introduced to, I needed to trust myself that I would recognize danger if and when it presented itself.

My friend and I entered the old, renovated barn's haymow. Lights were dim, tables spread out allowing for each reader's privacy. I was instructed to read the readers' bios that were provided and pick one or as many as I wished, then sign in for a time slot.

"How do I know?" I asked.

She replied, "You will know," and bounced off.

"Gee, thanks for the help."

The bios meant nothing to me. I had no idea what I was to look for. Biting the bullet, I picked two people: one was an animal card reader and the other a medium.

The young man reading the animal cards was helpful, and yes, the cards seemed familiar, but what did I know? I moved on to the medium when my allotted time arrived. She stood up and came around the small table, wrapping her arms around me, saying, "We have been waiting for you. All of us recognized you when you walked in."

This is weird. "Who has been waiting for me?" I asked, looking back at the door. Her arms swept out, indicating the whole room. *Oh, this is going to be interesting*, I thought to myself, with a snarky attitude.

She insisted that I will be working with my hands. Not a stretch since I already was. I told her my profession, and she insisted it wasn't that. She replied that I had healing hands as she held them in hers.

"What does that mean?" I asked.

She attempted to explain Reiki, but it went right over my head. She also said that I have a guide who appeared a year ago and has been walking alongside me. It was an ancient man that comes from the Southwest.

Kokopelli, I thought to myself.

She continued on with my stepping into my "calling," and said life would take some curves, but I was stepping into only the beginning.

I asked, "How will my husband take this?"

She thought for a moment, responding that he has always supported me in my adventures.

"What about my children?"

"Your sons know you follow a different drummer, so it will not be a surprise."

Two out of two—not bad.

Then she looked into my eyes. "The three children that are living with you; their mother has decided to live. They will be a part of your life, but you will not be the main caretaker."

Now she had my attention. Not once did I mention my family, my friend, or her children. Our time was coming to a close when she said, "There is more that I must tell you," as she stopped the timer. "In the next several months, you will be told that you carry a great light. It will come from three people you don't know or know only on the surface."

In a few short months, three different people, who didn't know each other, randomly said to me, "You carry a great light."

My head began to spin with racing thoughts and recent conversations. How can this be possible? I couldn't dismiss the warmth radiating from my heart and the comforting thought that I may have something more to *be* in the world. Taking a breath of acknowledgment, trusting this new path was taking root, all I needed to do was trust the process.

That word again—*trust.*

Trusting the process was easier said than done. A rumbling of discontent was a daily companion. I was tired of not fitting into the mainstream workforce, and it was exhausting. People were exhausting to be around! Surface conversations, complacency, and contempt toward life were prevalent. I wanted more.

Here it was, being laid out before me. The choice between standing still or moving forward. Moving forward was the only option for my soul's development. Showing fear made me weak. One thought at a time, one question answered at a time, and stepping into and onto the path that I had laid out for this lifetime's journey.

Chapter 7
From the Journey to the Canvas

Gary and I traveled to Reno, Nevada, not to gamble, although his traveling bowling companions and their spouses did. We rented a Jeep, taking off sightseeing after they had completed their national bowling competition. Heading southwest, we stopped at Cartwright's Ponderosa Ranch, where the TV show *Bonanza* was filmed, along with the familiar surrounding towns. Circling Lake Tahoe, traveling along the mountain roads, standing in snow up to my shins in seventy-degree temperatures, and breathing in the wild pine scent, I felt a kinship to the land.

This wasn't unusual for me. I lived in the ancient hills in the Mississippi Valley Driftless region until I moved away in my late teens. The hills call me into their secret passageways, embracing and protecting me from the human world. It is the hills where I find my grounding and comfort. Here, I find balance and rejuvenation.

Our final destination for the day was Donner Pass. During the gold rush and the promise of a land now California, there was the promise of riches filled with milk and honey. The Donners were the last wagon train of the year. They were warned it was too late and that the unpredictable storms would trap them. Rather than wait out winter below, they were impatient. Ignoring the multiple warnings, they headed out and perished.

Before heading up the mountain road, we made a brief stop at a small Indian store that had caught my attention. It drew me in, pulling me to its secrets and stepping back in time with familiarity. I purchased a CD and left.

As we headed up the mountain pass to our destination, I wasn't sure what I was feeling. My heart felt heavy and breathing was labored. Mountain air is thin, and catching my breath and my usual stamina had been challenging on this trip. The high altitude had an effect, but something else was different.

We began walking around the grounds where the Donner Party had perished. I was rendered speechless. The deafening echoes of their fear, anger, hunger, and remorse vibrated deep within my body. Placing my hand on the boulder that was used for a wall of the shelter built in desperation, I was drawn further into the feeling of helplessness. Was I a part of the party? Or maybe I was open to feeling the whole of it.

Visiting the museum, we got a clearer understanding of how the wagon trains trekked over the mountains, the natural dangers from wildlife and the natives, and the extreme need to survive that turned to cannibalism. Silently, we headed back down to Truckee.

Again, the native store tugged at my heart. I needed to return to its comfort. I spent time walking around, admiring the jewelry, artwork, music being played overhead, and wanting to caress the drums. This felt like home. Peace washed through me, calming my soul.

Completing my final selections, I made my way to the checkout. On the wall over the cashier's shoulder, a picture at least six feet tall and four feet wide hung on the wall. Completing the transaction, she noticed how I was staring at it in wonder and suggested they could ship it home for me.

The second journey on my first introduction to shamanism retreat was that picture of the maiden in the white buckskin dress sitting in the wild grasses facing the deep, lush trees. How did I miss that painting on the wall just hours before?!

Tears pooled in my eyes. Something magical had begun to rise up from deep within; something I had buried. Was that me from another lifetime? Or was it a sign that I was being directed, and I was picking up the breadcrumbs along the way, allowing for my spiritual growth and awakening?

The answer to these questions was revealed in the late summer of 2025. In the advanced shaman studies, during an exercise to view the true souls of another, my partner picked up this same image. She further added that I was married to the chief, had children, and was revered by him and the tribe.

Chapter 8
The Karma's Agenda

The second shaman to enter into my life was Carole. She was a hypnotist, Reiki Master Teacher, and shaman. My two older sisters and I were in a weekend workshop with a variety of teachers and healers. Carole's shaman workshop was filled to capacity. It was she who provided my Reiki training and shaman services the following year.

A few months after receiving Reiki Level One and a shaman journey from Carole, I intuitively understood that the past is directly linked to the present day. In that first journey, my daughter, whom I had given up for adoption in this lifetime, was my daughter then. She was a toddler when I and the father, working in an open field in the mid-1800s with other settlers, were attacked by a local native tribe. I believed to have made a friendly connection with this tribe. The warrior I believed was a friend threw his lance, lodging it into my back and straight through my heart, instantly killing the child I was holding while running for our lives.

Protecting the child in this lifetime, and the child then, was a direct karmic link. The circumstances in which I had found myself, unwed, deserted, alone, and with no viable way to support the both of us, made me think I was unprepared to be the mother she deserved. My sincere intention was to give her a chance and protect her from poverty and my dysfunctional family and life. The fears I held were rational, and yet the karmic energy pattern played into my decisions. Protect her I must; I wasn't good for her.

I barely remember a time when there wasn't a deep physical burning pain on my back behind my heart. Massage therapists, healers, and electric current therapy did little to release the subscapularis muscle that felt like, and that I often described as, a twisted rope. At times it burned like a hot poker knife had been driven in. I learned to live with it.

A decade had passed when I began to ask: Who is friend or foe, and who is the warrior now?

The pain in my back was exactly where the lance was buried in my body from my first journey. It was then I began to ask Carole for her assistance. Several journeys began to reveal a pattern of betrayals with poisonous darts in my back, being shot in the back, and being buried alive.

Who are they now? Who was I then, to have caused the betrayal? Did it matter? It wouldn't change the past, but it could change the trajectory of my current relationships.

The classes and mounting stacks of books had opened a whole new world of possibilities. The silver thread of wisdom connecting everything together was simply love and forgiveness. By practicing blessing those who were creating havoc in my relationships and setting healthy boundaries, my physical body was responding. The pain in my back disappeared.

I know who the karmic players were and have no need to tell anyone. This was on me. This lifetime, my purpose is to clear as many karmic debts as possible.

1) Acknowledge with gratitude.
2) What energy is bleeding through?
3) Do I want to repeat it? No? Then seek ways to step away from that individual. Boundaries!
4) Bless them, hold the Light—with no agenda other than one day they may see.

The shaman's journey is equivalent to the art of journeying into the Akashic Records, where curses, contracts, and more can be addressed and transformed.

Chapter 9

Healing Touch Training Wakens the Slumbering Soul

It was my sister Marilyn's and my Level Four Healing Touch class, the last class before we began our certification process, if we chose to. We wanted that certification. For the next year, we would be working with a certified mentor and completing certification requirements. Our completed packets would then be sent off to be reviewed by the Board of Directors. We had already begun our classes for the animals.

In previous classes, I had become aware that when Marilyn and I were on the table as the patient with separate teams, we mirrored each other. This particular weekend, it became a detriment to my health. A migraine developed on Friday morning. I was determined to clear it, but nothing was working. Even one of the facilitators failed to make a dent.

We had been given teams of two for the weekend. Our assignment was to assess, treat, and document our findings and provide resources when needed. It was late afternoon on the second day, and both of us were the "patient." Sitting up on the table after my session, while my teammate wrapped up the session notes, we noticed several of the teachers crowding around Marilyn's table. Watching with interest, we waited patiently for other teams to finish. The facilitators stepped away as she stirred and became aware of her surroundings.

During the sharing of experiences and reporting our assessment as if we were sitting around the table with our colleagues in a professional consultation, a light went on. Our assessments were identical! While she had traveled outside her body during the spiritual surgery and was having difficulty returning, unaware of what was happening, I was picking up and carrying her energies on the physical plane.

I was an empath.

A new plan developed: I will not be on the table when she is.

Many have said that Marilyn and I sound alike, once unintentionally fooling her son. It wasn't uncommon to be heard talking in a crowd and be sought out by someone who thought I was her. A friend once called us bookends or twins born thirteen years apart. It's only normal, then, that we were energetically mirroring each other, except that it appeared to be one-way.

Marilyn noted that some of my recent health concerns actually mirrored her emotional situations. I had my doubts. For one thing, we lived ninety miles apart. My migraines were a thirteen on the Richter scale from one to ten. Granted, I was menopausal, and we had a family history of migraines on both sides of our parents, but it was the stress headaches that gave it away. I knew the difference. When the stress headaches appeared, she was struggling emotionally with her life issues.

It took me years to learn and incorporate grounding and protection techniques that worked for me. Carrying other people's emotional baggage is not healthy and is not a requirement to display as concern. It doesn't make you more special; it makes you sick.

Empathy vs. sympathy: Boundaries within relationships and boundaries within the energy realm are vital and go hand in hand. No longer do I leave myself open to the world's energies.

When I am working with others, I often pick up what is going on within my body. The first two questions I ask are: "Have you been feeling _____?" and "Have you had _____ lately?" Then I acknowledge the signal my body has given and dismiss it because it isn't mine to carry.

When I am feeling "off," I ask, "Is this mine?" When it's not mine, I ask if it's someone I know. If yes, I go through the possibilities. If I don't know them, I then send the individual a blessing and separate from it.

A blessing is different from sending energy.

I have to be careful when I am out in public, as I oftentimes forget to lower the shield and read the room. I find myself driving in the city without fear of who or what is around me. I pay attention, of course, but fear isn't my companion, discernment is. What you fear often becomes your reality.

The hermit in me avoids large crowds, enjoying the sanctity of my cave. As a child, I had learned that showing fear made you weak. Also, there is a difference between being fearful and observant. Fear can be blinding and keep you hostage from living. Observation is reading the room by taking notes, not judging, and managing how you navigate with respect and confidence.

The practice of listening to the inner voice and the one that I hear outside my body was often hit or miss. I learned that the voice outside my body was clear and direct, and that was the one to sit up and pay attention to. When I began my introduction into the healing modalities, Spirit spoke directly to me in that clear, direct voice.

Intention alone, that is allowing the energy to go where it needs to go, wasn't enough for the work I was being led to. I was to learn how the body works, how one organ is connected to another, and how the mind, body, and spirit work as a unit.

When sharing the "voice" speaking to me, it was often not taken well and met with raised eyebrows of concern, followed by asking for an explanation of what the voice was, leaning toward me being psychotic.

My education in the healing arts stretched my knowledge of how the body responds to thought, music, and color. I learned how to feel the energy patterns and the connection between the big toe and the crown. Swollen ankles were connected to disease in the body, and there was an energy pattern to a migraine and its possible causes. Go to the cause by backtracking and not looking at the symptom alone.

How often do we hear complaints about Western medicine treating the symptoms and not finding the cause? All the time! Energy medicine, if it is to be taken seriously, requires that the more you know, the more effective you will be.

Ethics was repeated in every class. Always ask permission from the person or the owner of the animal and property. Otherwise, it's an invasion of the energy body.

An example is that Cindi and I were providing a demonstration with a dog that was emotionally shut down - physically shaking, tail tucked, head down, and ears back - at a convention. My heart went out to this boy. He was afraid and surrounded by hundreds of people in a gymnasium. A plethora of vendors for animal rescues and merchants had gathered for the two-day event. They were well-intentioned people, not understanding that socialization for animal or human isn't exposure to large events.

The rescue group gave us permission to work with him after we explained our work. Before we started the demonstration, we asked people to remain in observation mode, and we explained what to look for in his body language. As I worked with him, sometimes hands on body and other times off, Cindi explained what I was doing over each point and each position. The audience easily observed his body language and facial expressions.

Nearly halfway through our demonstration, both Cindi and I noticed the dog feeling unsettled. Looking around for an explanation, we saw that a well-intended Reiki practitioner was directing energy to the dog! She was invading the dog's energy field and mixing with my work. This is unethical. Her intention was to help. She was walking by, saw the dog, and decided it was for her to help him, but it had a visible adverse effect on the dog. We had to start over.

Good intentions without information or permission can cause harm. Always ask before you send or provide a service: *Can I? May I? Should I?* Be sure you know that you are hearing your guide versus your ego. I will be honest; this is a trigger of mine. Interjecting what you *think* is needed is ego driven.

Here's a thought to consider. Multiple people sending energy to an individual can be detrimental to that person. Energy overload is a real thing. Sending it in a bubble so they can draw from it when and if needed can also be an overload. "Energy goes where it's needed" is true but consider that too much energy can become congested.

So, ask yourself: Why are you sending energy? Is it the only thing you know you can do?

Get permission first.

Chapter 10

I Am at the Wrong Bird Feeder

That summer was riddled with turbulent decisions and actions centering around three young children, their ill mother, and an employee. Working and attempting to build a healing center along with running a household, I was running on fumes.

"Our thoughts become our reality" was taken to a level of judgment. Compassion for those with illnesses, injuries, or drama was replaced with the belief that it was a result of negative thoughts creating it. We were to focus on positive thoughts and ignore the gnawing within the gut. Set your sights and intentions on what you want, and it will happen. If it doesn't occur, obviously you allowed negative thoughts to sabotage your objective. The ego was always blamed. Following intuition was set aside, and prophecies ignored for fear they would be brought into fruition. The "new age" movement took off like a cult. Positivity was warped into ignoring the unpleasant. This had to be difficult for guides, angels, and Jesus, who wanted to warn us about impending danger ahead.

The first message I chose to ignore came early that summer: *Be aware of poison ivy.*

While on a family vacation in northern Wisconsin visiting waterfalls, on our first hike of the day, I spotted the plant. We were in a field of poison ivy that led to the narrow trail. I followed behind as our sons and their young families had taken the lead. Horrified that the five adults and four children under five had just been exposed, my first thought was to stop everyone. Then reasoning set in. Why should I scare everyone and bring a halt to the day? The decision to remain silent and use the tools I had learned was put into action. Energetically, I visualized each person and cleared their energy field and body, then placed a shield around each one.

At the end of the day, I shared with Gary what I had done. His first reaction was alarm, then quickly relaxed, trusting my skill. Even though he didn't understand how it works, he was aware of the results. Everyone walked away from the weekend unaware of the danger they were in.

Throughout the summer, the same message of being aware of poison ivy and relationships sat at the edge of my thoughts. It was mid-September 2007. Life appeared to be happening around me while I stood on the outside, observing from a distance. Projects I had been working on since what felt like forever fell apart. Those whom I thought were in sync with mutual goals decided I was no longer a good fit. Rather than being forthright, they manipulated and violated my personal energetic field through the use of a new technique for clearing out what no longer served. The teacher was actually assisting them with good intentions but with deceitful patterns. Rather than speak with me directly, they messed with my energetic field and lied about it.

My thoughts and my gut felt the shifting energy around my connections with the group of women. When attempting to share what I was feeling, I was told I was focusing on the negative and to think positive. One major lesson learned is that I instructed my guides and God to place protection around me and that no one has permission to interact with my personal space without my verbal permission.

The awareness that came to light during my boundary-setting years wouldn't be forgotten. How quickly I forgot the importance of listening to the gentle inner voice of Spirit reminding me to listen to *all* messages. Some are warning signs of impending danger ahead. Take notice and adjust your speed: curves ahead, flashing yellow lights, proceed with caution. STOP! I was caught up in the words of those around me. I didn't listen to the voice within. I was paying attention to the outside crazy voices so I could be a part of a community.

Late summer, I began to recognize my responsibility. I wanted a community. To have that community, I needed to conform to their metaphysical rules. The first several weeks of being separated from those I thought were friends were difficult. I was beating myself up, angry at them for their deceitful ways and wondering why this was happening. As my head cleared, my bruised and broken spirit began healing. While it was difficult, I had learned from other unhealthy relationships how to reestablish boundaries and respect the experience as a learning tool, or so I thought.

On Labor Day weekend we took on a project of clearing the underbrush, saplings, and weeds that bordered the wooded property line. The message to pay attention to poison ivy once again entered my thoughts. In the past several weeks, during hikes with our dog, ivy was present. After the hike, I washed her down and my clothing, cleared and blessed, as I had done during our vacation. My internal thoughts questioned why I was bringing poison ivy into my life in the first place. Why couldn't I just let it go?

We spent the day digging and uprooting the unwanted plants, being vigilant for the dreaded poison ivy. I saw nothing. In the middle of the night, I woke up to the unrelenting itching and burning on my arms. The following morning, the rash had developed. Knowing it wasn't poison ivy, I knew it had to be an allergic reaction to an unidentified weed. I took another shower with disinfectant, which was the wrong thing to do.

Within twenty-four hours, I was screaming in pain. Blisters had appeared on my arms, legs down to my ankles, neck, back, and one dangerously close to my eye. The ER doctor insisted it was a severe case of poison ivy. I vehemently denied the presence of poison ivy in the yard. He insisted he knew better, sending me on my way contagious and in pain. Poison oak was my next best guess.

What in God's name was I supposed to learn from this?

Bandages became my friend and a source of laughter through gritted teeth. I resembled a mummy in makeshift fabric in Winnie the Pooh design. Bandages irritated the blisters more than comforted. Wrapped in the softest fabrics, my weeks were spent sitting on a white sheet protecting the furniture in a house smelling of oils. My days consisted of waddling from the covered couch to the bathroom to the washer and dryer, and repeat. That was the length of my activities. The blisters oozed and spread and would infect others that came in contact with anything I touched. Bedding, towels, furniture coverings, and bandages were washed daily.

The sun rays in the fall gave way to cooler air, allowing me to venture onto the deck for short periods of time. The young hummingbirds practiced their sword fights with each other and aerial acrobatics, swishing and swooping around me. These two youngsters were different from the other young hummingbirds in the past. They were interacting directly with me! I felt the vibration of their wings across my face and shoulders. Hovering what felt like inches from my face, the vibration of their beaks tingled my third eye. I leaned to the right or left, and they moved with me, a sacred dance.

Intrigued with what the message of their appearance might be, and maintaining the idea that everyone and everything around us, including the animals, are mirrors into our actions and thoughts, I began researching the meaning of hummingbird.

At first glance, the message of joy and love stood out. I had been manipulated and violated, feeling lost and disrespected yet again by those I trusted. My emotions were raw. Blisters left my skin raw. Hovering and dancing with me remained a mystery. Days passed, and the true message evaded my understanding. Those two little sword fighters kept showing up as if they were attempting to drill the message into my third eye. In my frustration of trying to "think" my way into the message rather than allowing my heart to receive, on the fourth day, tucking the soft sheets around me as I settled into the comfort of the couch, the prayer was sent forth.

"Oh, Spirit of Light and Love, the voice of wisdom and clarity, if there is anything more I am to recognize about the Hummingbird's message, please make it clear to me. Because I am not getting it."

Closing my eyes, I hoped sleep wouldn't be evasive again because the healing blisters had been interfering with rest. Over the course of the last week, the burning had dissipated and the itching waking me up after three hours of sleep. The lack of sleep, with the body healing, was exhausting. Everything in the past thirty days had been exhausting. Oops, there goes that negative wordage again. Well, sometimes just figuring out life and the players' motives is exhausting!

At four o'clock I awoke with an excited start. How did I miss the clarity of the message? My heart beat with excitement and peace, filling every cell of my being. I was at the wrong feeder! People have carried judgment regarding my animal spirit guides of Eagle, Wolf, and Hawks, which are all predators, to be exact. Oh, how precious are the songbirds that just bring a joyous attitude in song. I was seen as a predator!!!

- *Hummingbirds' food is the nectar from the plants. They don't feed or hang out at the seed feeders.*
- *Hummingbirds associate and play with each other. Their beaks are like swords; sword of truth.*
- *Hummingbirds have two speeds: fast and sit. They move forward, backward, sideways, down, and up in one graceful movement. They hover, play, swoop, dive, and soar to great heights. Adaptable to change.*
- *Hummingbirds are loved from a distance and feared up close. Watching them at the feeders is different from feeling the vibration of their wings up close and personal. Their beaks resemble swords and needles that can, if believed, drill into you faster than you can defend yourself.*

- *Perseverance and resilience symbolize strength. They migrate long distances and have to overcome challenges along the way. In many Native American cultures, the hummingbird is believed to be a bearer of light, joy, and love.*

  -Native American Tsa`Kan: The Flame that Dances Between Worlds.

How am I similar to the hummingbirds? My energy is similar, as I have been told I have two speeds. My activity level has been compared to the Energizer Bunny. I have the ability to adapt to change. I am loved from a distance and feared up close. My energy and passion exhaust people. My ability to work with difficult people and their needs by uncovering the core issue has become popular with other healers. These difficult cases are referred to to me; thus, the beak is the sword of truth.

Chapter 11
The Pledge to Overcome a Fear

My fear of snakes was irrational, and I knew it. If I was going to be working with animal behaviors, then I needed to deal with mine. My declaration was simple. I will get over my fear of snakes this summer. Gary and the boys, now young adults, gave me that look of humored doubt. With my intention set, I envisioned coming across snakes and calmly walking away.

It was a late spring evening when I decided to have a glass of wine. The kitchen was dimly lit. Casually selecting a glass from the cabinet, then reaching for the bottle of wine, I stepped on something cold. Stepping back and looking down, I saw nothing. Then, taking a closer look, it was blending in with the multi-colored rug. Bending over even closer, the recognition of the offense revealed a dead snake.

Instantly screaming "Snake!" in pure terror, in a single bound I flew over the small table in the kitchen and over the extended island. In a second bound, I leaped onto the safety of the couch, my backside planted on the back support with my bare feet tucked under the cushions, screaming, "Snake!"

Gary looked at me with a "what the heck is your problem?" expression. Again, I repeated, "Snake!"

His calm, dismissive response was "There is no snake."

Slapping the back of his head, I repeated, "I stepped on a snake!"

Reluctantly, he meandered to the kitchen and came back holding a large dead garden snake. "You mean this little thing?"

It was surmised that either one of the cats, Sassy or Spencer, had delivered the gift. I am a barefoot gal, so for the next few weeks, shoes or socks were worn religiously. Eventually, rational thinking returned, and I focused on my initial intent to face my fear head-on. Rather than freak out, as I did prior to stepping on the dead snake, I set a clearer intention for myself to start talking calmly to them and observing their skin patterns and movements. It was time to honor the gift nature was obviously ready to deliver.

Immediately, every snake in the county came to my aid every single day! They appeared in the middle of a parking lot or resting on stone driveway walls in perfect alignment with my car door. They slithered across my path on the sidewalks, and let's not forget to mention my yard. My intention was heard loud and clear, and I was being taken seriously.

Upon waking each morning, I wondered where the next opportunity would appear. With each opportunity, I was becoming more comfortable with their sudden appearances. You could say it wasn't sudden, as I was expecting them to present themselves. Once they appeared, I stood by my word and began talking to them, examining their skin texture and color patterns. I was creating a purposeful peace and respected connection.

By the end of the summer, I was proud of myself for a job well done. The intention was simply to overcome my irrational fear from an indoctrination of Biblical teachings correlating the connection between the serpent and the devil. Mother and my sister held snakes all the time. I had no time for them up until now.

On a late September day, the sound of the cat door opening caught my attention. Casually glancing over, I saw Sassy carrying in a pencil-lead-thin snake, twisting in protest, hanging out both sides of her mouth. Everything I thought I had overcome flew back in my face as the fear of a live baby snake lost in my house became a whole new fear.

Gary was working in the backyard when he glanced up, hearing my screams and panic while fleeing the house yelling, "Snake!" With one swift jump, I balanced on the deck railing, my feet tucked around the spindles and bottom brace. Behind me was a twelve-foot drop.

For someone who claims to be a track runner, a casual jog doesn't cut it between the seventy-five-foot distance between him and the snake. That snake could be anywhere in the house and locating it would be a miracle. "Get a move on it!" I screamed. His calm, dismissive smile irritated me even further; I wanted to make him pay dearly. How, I wasn't sure, but I *would* get even.

He entered the house, returning seconds later with the baby snake in his hands. Again, that smirk. Sassy had dropped it a few feet from the door. Spencer, my hero, held it down with his paw on its head, pinning it while it wiggled and twisted in protest.

A few hours later, it was time for a serious discussion with the cats, mostly Sassy. I thanked them for their gifts and for helping me move past the fear of snakes. I thanked the snakes, too, for showing up every day and everywhere. As much as I appreciated their gifts, from this moment on, there would be no more snakes, mice, chipmunks, or flying squirrels, dead or alive, brought into this house. There wasn't another animal gift, dead or alive, brought in after my well-stated request. Each morning before stepping across the threshold onto the deck, their gift lay waiting.

Moral of the story is that if you set an intention and truly mean it, it may manifest in ways you cannot predict. We often run from our fears, casting a darker shadow around them, building them into something more than what they are. What is holding you back in fear? Is it time to face that shadow that has become your prison?

All of the All is listening and waiting to serve you.

Chapter 12
Sedona: Reliving the Past in the Present

A group of us gathered together monthly, practicing mediumship and message circles, getting together for exploration and fun activities. A trip to Sedona was a *must-do*. Dawn hired her Shaman friend as our guide. A couple of days prior to our departure, Dawn called us together. She had been told she had a message for each one of us relating to the trip.

The message I received was that my guides were happy with my progression and that a gift awaited me. It would be under some brush and beside a red rock. Anyone who has been to Sedona knows that it's *all* red rock!

Our first outing began in the beautiful Wet Beaver Creek Canyon. Introductions to our guide and his partner were made. They looked familiar, yet placing where and when was filed away in my memory.

Beginning our hike into the canyon, I had gone maybe forty yards when I stopped short. The memory of my first meditation came flooding back. The canyon slope to my left was familiar as I had flown over it on a day much like this with blue sky and scattered clouds stretched over the canyon of dead trees. A few feet more, and there was the tree I had landed on, overlooking the canyon floor in contemplation. Contemplating what, exactly, I wasn't sure, but I knew I was alone.

Anticipation began stirring first in my solar plexus and heart. My soul knew this trip was important. This trip was the closure of an old chapter with a new one about to begin. Then it clicked that our guides were the facilitators from many years ago at my first retreat when I met Kokopelli and the Indian maiden dressed in a white buckskin dress! This was not a coincidence.

Keith and Sulanna led us deeper into the green canyon, stopping along the way to teach the shaman's way of how to speak with nature and animals, gifting us with Sulanna's handmade medicine pouches.

The plan was to cross a small stream, spending the day on an island. Arriving at the stream's crossing, we saw that a late spring snowmelt had turned the trickling stream into fast-moving currents. Keith explained that it could sweep a car down the river, making it too dangerous to cross.

Several of the leaders talked it over and decided we were going to cross by making a human chain. Keith and

Sulanna tried to stop us since they didn't want their charges swept away in the icy waters. Taking off our shoes, one by one, we stepped into the knee-high rushing water, taking the hands of those taller and stronger, creating the human chain. It was my turn, followed by three people after me.

Respectful memories of my childhood were about living by a river that flooded yearly, wiping out everything in its path as it roared into life. I knew its power. On the other side, those who had crossed encouraged us. Stepping into the cold water, I felt the riverbed beneath my feet. One step after another, I walked across, not taking the outstretched hands. Climbing onto the riverbank, I noticed my knees weren't wet. The voices of my party began to drift into my awareness, saying that I had simply walked across the water.

All of us, safely on dry land, dried our feet the best we could before putting our shoes on. Keith was astounded at our determination and fortitude to overcome. The morning was filled with shamanic exercises and discussions.

Midday, we sat down for a bite from packed lunches under the canopy of trees, some alive and others dead. It was beautiful and peaceful all at the same time. Keith informed us we had two more exercises before heading back.

Given instructions, I felt the pull to walk to the south end of the island, where the two streams met into one. A pile of brush from years of flooding mountain snow blocked my passage. Determined, I climbed over the twisted dead branches, carefully watching my foot placement and balance. Moving and shifting branches as needed, an interesting piece of driftwood became exposed.

Pulling it out and examining it, images of ancient people and animals were visible. Turning it over, the driftwood held the image of a horse's head with a flowing mane. Driftwood is nature's masterpiece, and this one was stunning. Its weight and size would be burdensome to carry with me. Setting it against a tree, I whispered that if this were meant to be mine, it would be here when I returned.

Climbing up onto the red rock boulder, facing the juncture where the two streams met, I watched the merging waters pick up energy, swirling in a vortex pattern before heading downstream peacefully. Our assignment was to look for and communicate with the faeries and anything else that would listen and respond.

Sitting on the red boulder, I wondered if I would get anything. At the juncture where the two streams joined, an image of a Native American man and woman appeared.

They waved in acknowledgment. Telepathically, I heard them praise me for the work I had done. They nodded and disappeared.

Okay, am I imagining this?

I heard the signal to return to camp. I went back over the brush pile, where the driftwood waited for my return. Before carrying it out, I asked if it belonged to me. Doubt was a constant companion. My childhood taught me that receiving gifts was for others, and I was selfish to expect one for myself. Was this really meant for me, even though it was under some brush near a red rock, just as Dawn had indicated?

The following day we traveled to Loy Canyon, hiking for two miles and climbing a mountainside to a shaman's cave. I had woken up with a migraine. The many vortexes may have triggered it, and although I carried medicine for this affliction, the side effects would render me weak and lethargic. I chose to tough it out, hoping it would pass.

Driving up the mountain, viewing the hieroglyphics carved into the red stone by forces of nature, I was in awe, but the migraine wasn't lessening. If anything, it was getting stronger. *God, how am I going to do this?* I wondered.

Stepping onto the paved parking lot, I looked around at the incredible green mountainside reaching into the clouds. We began our three-mile hike, crossing dry runs, going under and around brush and low-hanging trees. Keith continued teaching us the ways of the land. With eyes closed, we felt the heartbeat of the land beneath our feet, walking both forward and backward, trusting our intuition by feeling the voice of the land talk to us.

We entered the grounds of the ancient trees, which were a thousand years old but no taller than twelve, maybe fifteen feet. The closer we came to the base of the mountain trail, the more my body ached from the migraine. It reminded me of the worst ones I had before I was diagnosed. *Oh, this isn't good,* I said to myself. I prayed and implemented Healing Touch techniques I had learned for migraines. Nothing worked.

We rested on a large stone shelf where ceremonies were held, both current and generations past. Just before I reached the shelf, I told Stacey that I had died there. "It wasn't a murder," I said. "I just died here."

Still higher we climbed, until we reached a stone ledge approximately four feet wide that wrapped around the mountain wall. Below the tilting, smooth stone walls, the trees were barely visible. I sat down cross-legged, overlooking familiar land. Even with the migraine, I felt peace.

Dawn began to sing in native tongue. Jeffrey played the didgeridoo around each of us. Someone played a flute. I drifted into an altered state, viewing the life I had lived in this sacred place generations ago. Two others in the group had lived here too. We were shaman sisters. We were healers. The first shaman journey taken with Keith and Sulanna had come full circle.

Who the other two were, I wasn't sure. I knew we were shape-shifting out of our human bodies. I failed to shift before landing on the stone shelf below. The music stopped. Dawn shared that two of her sisters had lived here. When our work was complete, we had shape-shifted off the ledge—Dawn, Dianne, and me.

Why didn't I shift out of my body? I asked silently. I doubted. I had listened to my sister of origin, who doubted everything. I have traveled many lifetimes with this, repeating the pattern. Doubt and trust are linked together.

It was time to descend. My whole body was screaming in protest. *How am I going to do this safely?* The silent answer was *Trust.*

Reaching the stone shelf where I had landed, every bone in my body felt broken, my head reliving the fractured skull of the slow death eons ago. The pain was crippling. I wanted to cry. I wanted to crawl under a scrub brush and die.

Joel and James found me curled up in a ball. They were concerned since I looked like death warmed over. I whispered to them that I had died here. Dianne and Dawn rushed over after seeing Joel beckon for assistance. Others came, sending Reiki, but it only made things worse. I asked them to stop.

Dianne, for the first and only time, saw all the broken bones, as did James. Together, they energetically put me back together while Dawn, uncharacteristically commanding, told me to focus on her while they worked. Unsure how long it took, whether in present or quantum time, our guide called for our trek back. My body was weak. If it weren't for Joel and James walking on either side of me, or when needed, in front and behind, energetically holding me up, I don't know how I would have made it.

The trees were talking to me, congratulating me for my progress. I raised my hands, palms up, acknowledging I heard them and accepting the recognition.

The following day we headed out to a national park for leisure. Although weak, I was stronger than anyone expected or hoped for. Diane, Joel, James, and I headed out, walking the paved trails, standing on the cliff's edge with arms spread out, faces tilted to the westward winds. We played with the vortexes and embraced the sacred land.

Standing on the ridges of the canyon we were walking, I saw in my mind's eye many tribes standing with their weapons held high in honor. I began speaking out loud their messages. If only I could remember what they had said. I knew one day it would be revealed to me again when it was time.

A revered Shaman was visiting the area for a short time, and there was to be a gathering that night to hear and meet him. James insisted that I needed to meet the Shaman after he had spoken. For the life of me, I couldn't understand his insistence. Joel on one side, James on the other, we walked over, standing in line until it was our turn.

The Shaman stopped, looked at me, and said, "We have been waiting for you."

The familiar sense of confusion with his recognition flooded my senses. He spoke directly in both English and native tongue. I had fallen into a trance. His lips were moving, words were being spoken, words I recognized yet was unable to retain. Why could I hear, understand, but not retain?

The following day we were leaving for home. I wanted to remain. The driftwood that was gifted to me had been placed on our fireplace mantel upon our return from Wet Beaver Canyon. Everyone saw different animals at different times. Bear, wolf, deer, raccoons, and ancient humans were the common ones. The horse on the back side always gave a rush of excitement. It was heavy. The luggage could only be fifty pounds, and it was forty-nine pounds when we left Milwaukee. I would have to pay the extra fee. It weighed in at exactly fifty pounds!

Arriving home, it was cold stepping outside the terminal. The March weather had begun to warm, but the air was shocking compared to Phoenix. The air was crisp, hovering between winter and spring. During our trek back home, with James driving, Joel and I sat back as passengers. We had shared a room together, two flights, and experiences not easily explained over a span of a week. Our lives had intertwined in more ways than one.

Our yard remained snow-covered, which wasn't unusual for living on a hill surrounded by woods. Standing at the kitchen sink looking out the window, an old fox came trotting straight towards the house. Thirty feet away, it took a sharp right and disappeared into the woods. We hadn't seen a fox in our yard until that morning and not since.

The old fox and the ancient ones provided a message that I didn't walk alone. This is where I need to be. This is where I need to grow.

The questions I began asking were difficult to wrap my head around:

1. If we have lived many lives in different cultures and different sexes, then how does our physical ancestry play in? Do we have a spiritual DNA?
2. Native people are proud of their ancestry, hating the Europeans for destroying their culture. What if *you*, the native, played the role of the soldier who wiped out your current ancestors? The Germans and the Jews; Palestine and Jerusalem; or white Americans versus other races?

The list continues to grow with each passing generation. When and what will shift humanity's need to condemn and overthrow others? This is where we, as young and old souls, begin to atone for our unknown past through the art of forgiveness and learning through experience. My faith was developing a thicker, yet more sensitive, skin. My soul was awakening and maturing.

Chapter 13

A Frozen Raven on the Wire

It was a Sunday afternoon in summer, returning from an in-depth Healing Touch weekend class with my sister Marilyn. We were exhausted. The classes were energizing and empowering food for the soul. My body, however, said sleep and assimilate the new information and bodywork for a few days. We arrived at her home around 6:30 PM and carried her luggage and books into the house, used the facilities, and said our goodbyes.

Opening the car door, I noticed something sitting on the high-line wire directly overhead. Concentrating and wondering what I was seeing, the bird wasn't moving. It appeared frozen in time. It wasn't any bird sitting on the wire, but a raven depicting the image of the Thunderbird or the Phoenix rising. I was drawn in, waiting, watching for movement that didn't come. The more I watched, the deeper I was drawn into a trance.

Marilyn needed to see this. Forcing myself to walk back into the house, she was shocked that I hadn't left. What felt like seconds had actually been a full five minutes. Where was my voice? Unable to speak clearly, I pointed my finger outside. She followed, wondering what was wrong. Directing her gaze by pointing my finger at the raven that still hadn't moved gave proof I wasn't hallucinating.

Immediately, she cupped her hands, palms out, directing energy outward and upward. White light streamed out, encapsulating the raven. Still in a trance state, I managed to place my hands together, following her lead. Nothing happened. I was rendered incapable of anything other than to watch. Within a minute or so, it seemed, the raven began to move, flexing its wings and flying off. However, its beak remained frozen open with its tongue still visible.

The trance began to wear off. Thoughts, though sluggish, started to formulate. I had so many questions, as did she. We saw what we saw. Marilyn took me back into the house, grounded me, making sure I was able to drive the hour and a half home. Why? What happened, and what did it mean? Was the high-line high voltage? Not likely as other birds had roosted there before and again the following day without incident. It was confirmed to be a telephone line.

Why was it in the shape of a Thunderbird, and why was I pulled into a trance?

It has been over twenty years since that experience, and still the "why" and the "what" remain. If I had a cell phone at that time or even a camera with me to capture it on film, I'm not sure I would have been able to. When I travel back to that experience, I slip back into a trance, although not as deep. Complete answers haven't been forthcoming as to the "why."

What I have learned since then according to the Native American Medicine Wheel is that I am born under the Thunderbird clan.

There was a span of close to twenty years where Marilyn and I had not spoken. I felt emotionally battered and worn down. Depression had set in. There were choices that had to be made and stood by if I were to become me again. She had gone in her direction, separate from mine, as we traveled our spiritual paths, coming back together stronger and wiser.

Chapter 14

When the Carp Called My Name

Sitting alongside the riverbank, waiting for the completion of the oil change, my mind began to drift upon all the changes and challenges since embarking on this new path. Classmates and friends talked about meditating and yoga and that everything is One. Meditating was frustrating. "Empty your mind," I was told, but my thoughts had a mind of their own. Yoga felt slow and boring. I vaguely understood the concept that everything belongs to the One. God created all things; therefore, God is in all things. Thus we are all related. I was in awe of what I was learning in Healing Touch, reading material, and allowing for the natural flow of my budding skills.

Settling into a comfortable position on the riverbank, I focused on the clear water flowing around the grasses in the middle of the river. I noticed the fresh green colors of the different grasses and how they moved with the flowing water, easily and effortlessly they moved in harmony. The taller wild grasses lining the riverbank stood still in the pool of water but swayed with the soft early summer breeze. The sensation of the water flowing gently and caressing my skin as it passed by felt real.

Is this a form of meditating?

Enjoying the experience, the splashing of water a short distance down the river to my right caught my attention. Thinking it was fish surfacing to feed on the insects hovering above the water's surface, I listened. Several more splashes occurred, sounding more demanding. Without thinking, I called out, "Are you calling to me?"

Several quick splashes followed in response.

Now was the time to put to the test what others had talked about in my classes. What if the fish felt my connecting with the river and was responding? What if it was actually trying to communicate with me? After all, it splashed several more times in response to my question, or was that only a coincidence?

Time to find out.

Telepathically, I asked him to swim closer so I could get a better look. Within seconds, a large carp swam upstream, stopping a few feet in front of me. Two coincidences?

Uncertain and curious, I chose to continue testing and observing the responses. My visibility to observe was hampered from where he lay in the clear, shaded area of the stream. Telepathically conveying that he was beautiful but in the shade, I asked if he could move into the sun. Much to my delight and shock, he shifted positions into the sunlight. The sunlight reflecting onto the water danced with sparkles above him, highlighting his beautiful scales.

I had never considered a carp to be beautiful because he is a scavenger, after all. He belonged to the river and lived as one with his surroundings. I was mesmerized. Asking if he had a mate, his reply was a swish of his tail, rippling the water's surface. "Could you bring her to me so I can meet her and enjoy her beauty too?"

He turned and was gone. Sitting on the bank, I thought I had a wild imagination when both of them stopped in front of me in the sun! How can this be happening? Yet here I am, talking to a carp, and it's responding to me! We basked in each other's company, just enjoying the knowledge that this is what being within the One means.

In the distance, the mechanic called out that my car was done. I extended a grateful thank you for their presence and the privilege of being called into their world.

More unlearning for me to do. I had judged this beautiful fish as a simple scavenger, like judging the snake as evil. Everything has its place on the planet. Everything has purpose and value. Humans rate themselves above all others, not realizing they belong to the whole universal One.

Chapter 15

The Man Upstairs Makes A House Call

Although I wouldn't be described as an angry person, unless you have missed or simply ignored all the signals I was providing in calm conversations and in a direct manner, underneath was a raging volcano. My entire life, I have given people excuses for their behaviors let it go, it's in the past, understand where they are coming from, or reasoning. In my early adult years, a minister had said to live by example for others to follow. In *A Course in Miracles* ministerial training, the same concept was applied.

The problem lay in the teaching that I needed to take responsibility for the dysfunction within these relationships because they were a mirror to my own reality. Hogwash. Yes, I believe life is a reflection. I also believe that within that reflection, you take responsibility and change what isn't working any longer. People are going to become upset when you stop playing the same role. The norm has changed, and they are now uncomfortable. Because the situation within a heartbreaking relationship had not produced a favorable outcome, it was my fault? The Inner Knowing at the core of my soul knew this perspective was false. Everyone has to take responsibility for their part of the storyline. I cannot be responsible for another person's actions; they have their own shadow work to address.

The split felt like losing a limb. Attempting to define myself was taken as trying to help. That wasn't my intention. I wanted the pain to stop by using my words and what I had been learning. Mourning the loss of this once-valued relationship, a deeper new depression began to set in. It was the deepest pain I had ever felt. My self-esteem had fallen to its lowest level. The vision held in my mind equaled needing two spotters to assist me in stepping up onto the curb safely. I had to love myself more to stop the insanity. Many spiritual people told me that this was selfish. If I had been practicing correctly—mirroring back to myself the dysfunction—the other person would follow. Judgment.

Struggling through the day, angry that I had lost family and friends, there were many who thought I was in the wrong. Only a few stood by my side. Following what I believed, what Jesus was directing me to do wasn't enough to calm the storm brewing inside. Late one afternoon, a friend was sitting with me in my car in her driveway. I cried with anger and frustration.

"Why is it so wrong of me to not want to be verbally assaulted? Why do I have to "put up" with the insanity within the relationship? Why am I the one who is always wrong and needs to listen up and make changes?"

After listening to my questions through the endless tears of anger and frustration, she asked if I trusted her.

"Of course I do."

"Then come into the house with me."

"No, your husband is in there!"

"Linda, do you trust me?"

Again, I replied yes.

"Then come in. We will go to a room far away from him."

I followed her to her bedroom. She grabbed a pillow and said, "This is Sara. Hit her."

"No, I can't do that!"

Of all the crazy things, she started to mimic back to me all the horrible, hurtful things that had been said to me. Hitting the pillow with both hands, she flew backward, landing on the bed. I was horrified at what I had done out of anger. Standing up, bracing herself, she started taking potshots at me. Again, with both hands hitting the pillow, she stepped back without losing her stance; she was ready.

The force and power of my striking out reflected the depth of my anger. It had no bottom, and it was ugly.

For days, that event replayed in my mind. Where is all this anger coming from? The depth of this monstrous anger shook me to the core. I'm mad at the injustice of it all. I'm mad at the lack of respect I wasn't given. I just want to be seen as an adult, not a child who needs to be set straight at every turn. Pardon me if you think I was trying to fix you, but I was trying to save myself.

The perfect storm had come. Walking into the house after a trying day, I broke down into righteous sobs, crying out to Jesus. "Jesus, if you are really out there, I need help because I can't stand this anymore."

In that moment, I saw Him standing in my living room. Looking twice, wondering if I was imagining it. "I'm mad," I shouted at the figure.

"You have a right to be mad," was the reply.

"I can't live with anger anymore! I'm going to spread a lot of hostile stuff into the universe if I keep this up." (The new-age concept that expressing emotions that weren't butterflies and kisses would harm the universe.)

“You’re hurting yourself if you don’t express these emotions. I have shoulders to carry your anger. Give it to me,” He responded.

I knew He was right. The next step was about faith and trusting, something I had become accustomed to practicing. Thank you, Kokopelli.

“On one condition, if I do have an explosion, I don’t want anyone around when it occurs.”

“Deal,” Jesus said with a confident smile.

The next six months, I experienced five to six explosive emotional temper tantrums daily. There were no rules to follow, and swearing was encouraged. I voiced with authority the injustices imagined against me, vomiting it up. In the eighth month, the temper tantrums had lessened significantly. Jesus’ presence felt like a parent holding their child’s hair back when sick, something I had never experienced, or maybe I just don’t remember.

“Jesus, I’m tired.”

“Don’t quit. You are almost there.” His voice was gentle with loving support, encouraging me to keep going.

Weeks had passed when, driving on the freeway, the familiar rage began to bubble to the surface. Crying, with vulgar and judgmental language spewing forth, I screamed that they needed to take off their rose-colored glasses. A miracle occurred, for in that instance, the realization came that I needed to remove mine first! Laughter erupted. Genuine peace and joy began to fill every cell. A breakthrough, as promised.

My body was storing everything I had ever experienced, despite my best efforts to find healing through humor. Everything I tried to let go of and move on from was waiting for my attention. I tried showing everyone that I was worthy to carry it all. It was the belief that this was my cross to bear, just like Jesus carried the cross for us. Well, that is just BS! Everyone needs to take responsibility and stop blaming God and others for the choices made. Free will was given to us. God and Jesus are not the marionettes in our lives.

Many of us were taught to have "suck it up, buttercup" attitudes. Get over it! I will give you something to cry about. Be a good little girl and hug your elders. You are so stubborn and refuse to listen. Pull yourself up by your bootstraps. These are the endless phrases spoken to me with the intent to make me stronger nestled into my cellular structure, mentally, physically, and emotionally.

The rotting anger I was given permission to expel felt like a form of exorcism. With a lot of work and guidance from my friend Jesus, I continue to heal and learn.

Trauma and drama play out in many forms. The concept that love is earned is the greatest thief of all. It seeps into other unhealthy beliefs. A baby should not have to earn love, nor should a child. If love is shown through harm or neglect to make someone stronger, the imprint is played out with feelings of not being good enough and takes up important space by always saying "I'm sorry." It shows up in your personal relationships by being afraid to say no, to say anything at all. How do you show love?

The imprint of my life experiences needed to be washed clean. Its imprint was in every cell of my body, waiting to manifest into a visible form, and had already done so in my relationship with self, but I hadn't realized it.

My shadow work had reached another level of understanding. Anger isn't the enemy but your friend when you choose to use it wisely.

Chapter 16
A Nudge from My Guide

Winter was beginning to set in. My bear energy was beginning to settle in for hibernation. I tended to curl up on the couch, wrapped in a blanket, watching Netflix with a dog snuggled beside me. Winter was the time to catch up reading a book from the stack on the desk or typing away on the laptop. It has been said you know when you are a writer when you need to write every day. Well, that isn't me at all! I have to force myself to sit down in front of the laptop and then search for words, so I don't sound like a child writing their first story. The view of the flower gardens from my windows had all been put to bed. Time to slow down.

This dark November day, a gentle stirring began to take form on the outer edges of my thoughts. I was restless and agitated.

Catching up on Zoom twice a month with Ellen in Tennessee, Pam in Arkansas, and Iris who lives in the next town over from me for social and book study. It was our ritual to begin the discussion with Pam opening the Four Corners, catching up with our lives, and digging into the chapter(s). Pam is a forever student, always expanding her knowledge. It had been a long time since I'd taken a class that stretched or even piqued my interest. Maybe that is what had me agitated.

That week, I began searching for possible classes and workshops, maybe a retreat was is order. Several retreats sounded interesting but didn't land as the direction to take. The common theme in the three retreats I gravitated to was based on shamanism. My search then led to local shamanism training. Boom—three came up, and all three within an hour and a half from me. Picking out two from their websites, I sent an email of inquiry. Windhorse Shamanic Services replied back stating she had a class starting in a few weeks!

Oh great, I would need a drum or rattle. Of course last year I donated all the rattles and an assortment of drums to the local charity store. Remaining was a flute and a drum. I hadn't mastered the flute, and the drum sounded like a thud. Both were hanging on the wall.

The web search for the perfect drum in my price range began. I placed the order in plenty of time for the first class. It hadn't arrived as planned. The night before the class, I reached for the old drum that, two weeks ago, still sounded like a thud even after applying the multiple tips for tightening the deer skin. Drum in hand, I wanted Gary to hear the thud. The first tap vibrated with a deep, resonating sound. Shocked, I tapped it three more time. Sure enough, it was responding. Was it waiting for me to step into a new direction? It was coming with me to class.

The new drum came and was waiting for me when I arrived home after class. The old drum was sleeping, awakening only when I was ready to hear the shaman's call.

About ten years ago, while reading a book about natural "healers", I recognized myself, and that I might be a shaman. I called Dawn. She laughed and said, "Yes, Linda, of course you are. What makes you think otherwise?"

"I'm not Native, and it would be wrong." was my reply. Impostor Syndrome was the imprint of my programing.

The following week, I made an appointment with a local shaman and psychologist, Dan Huber. Stepping into his office, I said, "I think I'm a shaman." His response was to take a journey and find out. He explained what a journey was and it will give us the answer.

Fifteen to twenty minutes later, he returned from the journey, stating, "Linda, you are a shaman."

Standing up I said, "Thank you. I will get back to you." and left. After digesting this information for a few weeks, I along with six others, began our journey into the world of shamanism in the dead of winter. Pam Kackelmeier offered her tepee. Wrapped in blankets, the fire blazing in the circle, I stepped through another door of awakening.

Entering Deb's class, under the assumption this would be a refresher course, I was mistaken. Dan had taken my stirrings and planted seeds that I wasn't ready to embrace fully years ago. Now I have had my wake-up coffee, so to speak. I was charged. Within the first fifteen minutes, I perked up, recognizing this was not a refresher course. Deb was going to take me deeper still into what I didn't think I knew.

We were given assignments and could practice or not, as it was our choice to make. Without the practice, we would receive exactly what we put into it. During my first journey assignment at home, my ancestors appeared. The intention I had set was for physical healing of the the pancreas. Generational aging diabetes had become my reality.

The medical treatment plan had created a war within my body. The side effects were absolutely worse then the disease. Thinking I had shingles, I went to the walk-in-clinic, only to be told it wasn't, but if a rash appeared, to return. It hadn't appeared but the pain on my torso wasn't lessening. Three days later, I returned to the clinic, suggesting it was possibly internal shingles. Again, the answer was no. What was causing the pain?

The doctor took some history, appearing to be concerned and wanting to get to the root cause. He ordered an X-ray of my spine for possible pinched nerve. After reading the report and viewing the X-ray, he prescribed more medication for a pinched nerve. The counter was beginning to look like a pharmacy.

My chiropractor took a look at the report, then had me come in for a treatment plan. He was going to treat me for sciatica! The X-ray had shown a slight compression in the hip socket, but that wasn't where the pain was. Both of us were a little disturbed that I was given medication I didn't need for an issue I didn't have. We began to backtrack about when the symptoms started, when the injections was increased, along with the past year's symptoms. The nerve pain began six days after the increased injection.

Over the course of ten-plus years, I had developed allergic reactions to antibiotics, high blood pressure medication and several supplements. A quick research on the injection medication indicated nerve pain as one of the side effects. There was an internal war going on. All medications were stopped right then and there. All the symptoms I had been complaining about over the year weren't severe enough to be taken seriously until now. Even then, I was warned about heart attacks, stroke and the list went on. To live longer this miserable wasn't worth it.

During the following six weeks, the only fabric I could tolerate against my skin was cotton. My ancestors' message was that this can be turned around. My assignment was to know what authentic love is. Does anyone know what authentic love is? I was open to listening and exploring what it was and in what form it shows up in.

Four months into my studies of practicing and reading everything my guides put in front of me, discovering what authentic love was, was elusive. The *I Am Word* series enlightened me on many levels. One being that love is an action word not a noun. My entire life, I didn't think I knew how to love because I believed it was a feeling. Love is action. Love is how you move in the world by not purposely causing harm to the inhabitants of the Earth.

I had also set the intention in my journeys to visit and commune with my animal spirit guides of the four direction.

Slightly shocked, Tiger appeared in the East. The past summer, I purchased a tiger key chain. I was already being prepared. To the South, Sturgeon appeared. According to the Medicine Wheel, I'm born under the Sturgeon. Bear appeared in the West. Several Native Americans had told me that I carry Bear energy. In the North, the Snow Goose, which is the feather used in writing and storytelling. Visiting each one, I was shown their native habitats, sights, sounds, smells and the importance of their presence. Bear wanted to be called *Happy.*

I asked him, "Why the name Happy?"

He replied, "Doesn't it make you smile inside and out?"

Yes it does!

He took me on trails foraging for food. When we arrived at the stream alive with salmon, I stopped. I don't like salmon, no matter how many ways it is prepared. Happy encouraged me to play in the water while he caught his dinner.

"Happy, my power animals and guides such as Eagle ans Wolf are feared as predators. They are killed as trophies and considered dangerous to man's survival. My experience, among others, is that I too am feared. Admired from a distance but feared all the same."

Happy responds, "Every living organism is a predator. The bird eats the worm, insects, seeds produced from the plants. The worm eats the soil. The insects eats the plants. The plants use the birds, soil and insects to produce more. How are they not a predator?

Time to redefine the word *predator*. A deep sense of relief, a fragment of the understanding of authentic love, settled into my heart space.

Chapter 17

Run, Linda, Run

My unlearning of the ways of the industrial age of capitalism had made space for the awakening of my authentic self. Financial success was elusive no matter how hard I worked. Upon reflection, looking back in time, it wasn't my driving force. It was a necessity to survive in a world where money was king. I was miserable and a failure in the typical workplace.

Having entered into our retirement years, we were comfortable with working part-time, enjoying the quiet, unhurried moments. The political climate had noticeably shifted from democracy and decency between the two parties to a chasm that made the Grand Canyon appear small. United we stand, divided we fall. Families and friends were divided over politics. Humanity had become political. Our country and the world were divided, angry, resentful, and fear-mongering energy swept over the land.

It was still a popular concept to focus only on what you want. Focus on the good. Don't entertain the negative thoughts. Don't listen to the news because it's negative.

Avoid the negative at all costs. The cost is greater than anyone could possibly imagine. There is a shadow side to all of us, personally and collectively. Ignoring the rumblings of others will not make them vanish simply because you wish it so. Like a small child placing their hands over their eyes, believing if they can't see you, you can't see them.

Becoming complacent, moving through the world enjoying your freedoms, has a price to pay. So, our comfortable partial retirement wasn't looking comfortable any longer. Our marriage of forty-nine years has had its struggles, especially in the past ten years. I needed more.

I needed more out of our relationship. I was awakening into my own self-awareness and seeing with a new pair of eyes how unauthentic my relationships were. His agreeing with me yet having no intention of following through on the agreement, while I waited patiently for it to be fulfilled, was a form of insanity. It was passive–aggressive behavior. When the *ah-ha* moment struck home, I realized I too was being passive–aggressive. My passivity I called patience. When the patience had run dry, the slow-burning resentment burst into flames.

The attempts to reconcile and shift the dysfunction were met with resistance. The rules had been changed. My expectations and limits had shifted, and I was not backing down. Standing firm in my convictions was met with the same passive–aggressive behaviors. This relationship energy was all too familiar. The difference? I was married to it.

One fateful event was the last straw on the proverbial camel's back. A conversation turned ugly when the truth of how I was seen in the eyes of someone I loved and respected, our son, was revealed. It was my fault we were in this position in our retirement. He couldn't see how the political climate was threatening our healthcare, Social Security, and stocks, thus possibly risking our home. If I had done things differently and worked in the world as a capitalist, then we would be better off financially. I spent money on education that didn't produce a bountiful income.

My heart sank, thoughts swimming in confusion. Turning around and looking directly at Gary, who was, as usual, standing a few feet behind me, I pointed my finger and called him to step up and take responsibility for his mistakes too. Our son sided with his father's mistakes. Anger and disgust simmered in my heart. A client was coming soon, and I had to pull myself together and end the conversation.

Several days passed. My heart ached with an intensity from the losses and alienation from my children that I don't care to go into, losses that crushed me to the bone, to the core of my soul. My conversation with my bestie over the restaurant table earlier that day had revealed that I needed to emotionally disengage from those who should matter the most. She was deeply concerned.

Returning home, another one-sided conversation with Gary unfolded as I explained how I felt: that when I die, my family will not mourn me. I'm not on the list of importance or respected. He tried to say that wasn't true. I wouldn't let him finish, as it isn't about what is true, it's about how I feel. I deserve more than what I have been receiving. Distancing myself from our sons is needed for my own self-preservation.

On the counter lay an envelope addressed to us as Mr. and Mrs. The return address only had the address of our eldest son. He hasn't spoken to me for nearly two years, a year for his father. Picking it up, I whipped it across the counter, telling Gary to open it. Taking another blow was intolerable.

He had already opened it before I returned home. It was our granddaughter's high school graduation. The invisible knife that had been embedded two years ago twisted.

"I guess they can't invite you without me now, can they?" I shouted at him.

"They want you," he said in a hurt tone.

"It doesn't feel that way. It hasn't looked that way with their actions, now has it? I'm not going to drive five hours to be in the enemy's camp. Besides, that is the day of my Shaman training class, and I can't make that up! If I have to choose, I choose me." I stormed out, needing to disengage from the twisting pain of the gaping wound of a hemorrhaging heart.

That evening, I spoke with direct, harsh, and truthful words, all of which I fail to remember, while Gary sat in his recliner as he listened. The words came out calm at first, then grew in intensity. His pallor turned gray, shoulders hunched over, head hanging, as my words shot hot knives into his soul.

I lost count of how many times I had to become angry to get attention, to be heard, to be respected. Forty-nine years of marriage, and once again we had come full circle. He pretends to listen and care when he just wants to pacify me, to run from the discomfort.

Standing up, I walked across the room, stopped, and screamed. Blood-curdling screams erupting from my toes upward. Every cell in my body was purging again. This time it was different. Before, I had verbally sworn out my anger. Now, it was the screams about which I had only heard. The dogs scattered. I did not care. This felt refreshing. The screaming continued.

After the last scream, tears began to pool in my eyes. I headed to my bedroom for an ugly cry. Folding into a heap on the floor, little thirteen-pound Klink, a corgi and chihuahua mix, sat cowering in the corner. Reluctantly, he came forward with my encouragement. Seventy-pound Natalie, a Catahoula Leopard Dog, peeked over the bed, questioning if it was safe to come out. Together, with their heads in my lap, they comforted me as much as themselves.

The realization hit. I remember only a few times in my entire life that someone had held me in comforting arms. No wonder I have no idea what authentic love is. I wasn't valued enough to be held; I was valued for what I brought to the table.

Maybe I always needed to be the strong one. Self-reliant. Show no weakness. That persona. Did I make it easier for everyone else to not see me as a person?

My sons are intelligent, amazing men who had become gullible and, in many respects, naïve, as I had been at their age. Gary is a good, kind, gentle man. He didn't believe me when I said that if we got a divorce, it would be said that he was a saint for living with me. How many examples had I given months before, supporting this fact? Five to be exact. At that time, he hung his head in agreement. Passive-aggressive people behind closed doors are emotionally destructive.

The tears shed, eyes red, heart yet again cauterized, I knew that leaving was my next move. Calmly, I picked myself up, patted and reassured my two comforting companions, and walked back into the living room. Neither one of us looked at the other, both concentrating on watching the television screen. Deep, painful lines etched his face. A gray aura, fear, and dread pulsed off of him.

Glancing over to speak my final words was a calm, shocking blow, and I didn't care. Never again would I allow this much disrespect to go unchallenged. At the core of my soul, it didn't matter anymore. I was alone. What became clear to me was just how alone I truly was.

Peaceful sleep followed me until morning. Plans were taking form. I was running away and letting a few people know my plans. Destination unknown—north, south, or west? East would land me in Lake Michigan.

The following morning, the laptop open, a steaming cup of coffee in hand, I caught up on a few emails and messages. Gary prepared for the day with no glances exchanged, just a numb wall of energy.

A few minutes before his departure, he stopped, leaning his back against the counter, arms and ankles crossed, facing me. I waited for him to speak. It didn't come. I finally ask,

"Do you need something?".

He began to say he had been up all night searching for ways to fix this. That he hadn't been a good husband and hadn't supported me in the way I needed and deserved. He said he would call our son and tell him he was wrong.

Stunned and a little impressed, I asked him, "How many times do I have to become so angry to be heard?"

"A lot," was his reply.

"My reserves are empty. I have nothing more to give or want to give. You and our sons will never hear 'I'm sorry' cross my lips ever again. Do you understand?"

He nodded his head in understanding. My thought was simple as he walked away: *It's a little too late.*

When I saw him direct the car down the road, I began gathering a week's worth of clothing, packed the cooler with food, and filled another suitcase with my drum, candle, sage, tuning forks, a selection of oils, and two oracle card decks—*Sacred Rebels* and the *Mystical Shaman* deck—along with working pens and my journal.

A note was left in the kitchen simply asking him to take care of Natalie and Klink. I knew that he would without a doubt in my mind. It was subtle, but clear. I had left and wasn't returning. With the car packed, I followed my ancestral spirits, guides, and trust, and turned the car heading west.

Chapter 18
Earning My Wings

I had no idea where I was being led. My emotional heart was torn out of my chest. Physically, it hurt, and I couldn't breathe. In the past few months, the shaman training sessions had awakened a deeper inner calling. Even with my battle-weary heart, I was more alive than I had been since my other classes and teachings. Why wasn't that considered valuable? Why am I disposable when no longer needed? Family can cut you into ribbons without even realizing it, or if they do, blaming others is justified.

Putting the miles between home and what lay ahead, my breathing normalized with my shoulders dropping, legs and back relaxing. Forty minutes out, I inserted my favorite CD, singing along off-key. Several of Garth Brooks' songs inspired and ignited a fire in my belly, more so now than ever before. *The Dance* speaks to my close family and friend relationships. If I knew how things would end, maybe I wouldn't take the chance, but what I learned from the pain is as valuable as the joys. *The River* encourages me to set my sail and let the river guide my dreams or sit upon the banks.

Oh, how I have set my sails outside the normal, and regret it not. It's better to try than not try at all. *We Shall Be Free* is a song of awakening to the needs of everyone, and until everyone is seen, heard, and respected, we will not be free.

Following the curves of the country road, breathing in the early spring air, sights, and sounds, *Standing Outside the Fire* begins to play. Rolling down the windows, turning the volume to a manageable decibel, my off-key voice joins Garth's. My right foot presses down on the gas pedal, picking up speed in rhythm with the energy. Tears trickle down my cheeks as I shout the words back to those I love, hoping they hear their folly and insensitivity.

A Rustic Road sign comes into view. Hitting the brakes, I make a right-hand turn. I was already on a detour a few miles back, guiding me to explore more roads. All roads do lead home, eventually, and they lead you to the discovery of the new. Once I was fearful of becoming lost. Over time, I realized I was lost without the exploration. Twisting around the tight gravel road corners, *Standing Outside the Fire* was on repeat. Singing or more accurately shouting, the joy of daring to dance inside the flame. I was inside the flame without regrets. I was free to be and to sail my vessel.

Finding myself in Viroqua, about twenty miles from the Mississippi River, this was my destination. The Driftless Region's hills called me home! Trusting my spirit guides, I secured a perfect lodging. I asked for two nights and was given the only rental kitchenette without asking. It hadn't occurred to me that one might be available. It was my home, my grounding, and my re-connection. Setting up my sacred space, I lit the candle, then cleared the space with my tuning forks. My guides had already cleared the space, waiting for my arrival. I emptied the cooler, set up the kitchen for my convenience, and was thankful I had brought coffee and coffee filters.

After a light dinner, I called my sister Marilyn to let her know I had landed safely. Then I pulled two oracle cards with the intention of gaining insight into where to go with my sons and husband.

Mystical Shaman Oracle Deck – The Serpent

- Time to shed the old, outgrown skin.
- Kundalini rising—passion, healing, and renewal offers the fruit from the Tree of Knowledge.

Sacred Rebel Oracle Deck – Free from Judgment, Free to Love

- The solution to family difficulties is being sorted out. Resolution will come to fruition soon.
- Relax, center, and settle into your body. Breathe the same as that which moves the trees.
- Water is blood, the same that fills the ocean, moves the phases of the moon. Feel the connection; it will connect with you.

Around eight o'clock p.m., Gary texted, asking me to let him know I was safe. I replied that I was.

Saturday, I headed out after opening the four directions, asking for assistance on my sacred journey throughout the day. Having no idea which direction spirit was taking me, I allowed myself to be led. The sacred Driftless Hills wrapped me in their energy, guiding me up and down unknown roads. Stopping to snap a picture of buildings from another time, a wooden bridge tipping forward on one corner, I felt the calming of my spirit before returning home on the following Monday.

Returning to my kitchenette in the early evening, I slipped into comfortable pajamas, called Marilyn to let her know it was a good day, and asked if I could spend Sunday evening with her on my way home. Then I lit the candle and proceeded to journal the insights I had received thus far. Afterward, I drew two more cards.

Mystical Shaman Oracle Deck: The Ghost Dance

- Honor and connect with ancestors and the living; otherwise, they will haunt us.
- Drum around your altar, ask for their wisdom. Write a new story.
- Bless and sage a photo of each, then send them off to the wind. Do not get caught in past lives or relationships.

Sacred Rebels Oracle Deck: Dream a Beautiful Dream

- Don't know how to fix or heal a current situation? It is what it is; nothing more can be done.
- Imagine what it is you want. Ask to see the beauty within it. Allow it to unfold.

Journeying helped me recall a past life with my son. It helped me understand the reason for our current life together. As for Gary, I had already set the change a year ago after an

Akashic record reading. The change was currently playing out.

More texts between Gary and me. It felt as if he was being truthful and taking responsibility. He was sorry and going to make it right. The screaming had emptied my emotional reservoir. Exhaustion was all that was left, and even that was slipping away into a dull, numb ache. Placing emotional distance between myself and them had to be done to survive. I did it before, and I can do it again. We will survive this. It will be different yet again, as it has been each time I shed skin that no longer fits. Others were not shedding their old skin, and that didn't matter any longer. I will take time for me; at the very least, two to three times a year. Void of emotional connection, I need to allow and trust that change was, and is, underway.

Sunday morning, I realized that I had been walking in a fog for the past few days. The kitchenette was cold. Try as I might to turn on the electric base wall heaters, I couldn't figure it out. I failed to notice the thermostat on the wall near the kitchen. The bathroom mirror was old, reflecting a distorted image, and was difficult to use. I thought maybe I should mention it to the owner.

Spirit responded: “You have a distorted view of yourself.”

Well, how could I argue with that?

It was time to open the four directions and take a journey, setting my intention for guidance. Paint, my spirit guide horse who takes me to the Upper World, stood in shallow water with clear blue sky and green grass reaching above the water’s surface. I heard the word “butterfly,” thinking Paint wanted to be called Butterfly. That was odd. Instead of traveling upward, she bounced around, imitating the flight of a butterfly.

“Oh! Butterfly is my guide today!”

Instantly, she landed on my back, wings spread across my shoulders. “You now have wings to fly,” she said.

With that, the three of us traveled skyward, reaching my sacred campfire where an Elder was waiting for me. I was instructed to dance and sing around the fire. Concerned about not knowing the steps, he instructed me to feel the flow of energy. Soon, my legs and feet moved swiftly and gracefully. My arms joined in, then my voice. I felt free.

“Why, Grandfather, couldn’t I speak in tongues?”

“It wasn’t your language. You have wings to fly; your feet will lead the way. You have chosen to walk alone.

Shamans do that. They have friends and family, yet their path is solitary. Go spend more time away from people, like Jesus did. Like all shamans did before you."

Traveling back to the Middle World, I thanked Paint and Butterfly, then turned to leave. I returned to my sacred space, on top of a hill overlooking an ocean with bear on my left, fox and others to my right. Fragments of my lost soul, pieces of my identity, were returned to me. Viewing and feeling the fragments of my spirit leap into my body, flowing in harmony. An initiation?

My running away had become a Vision Quest.

Setting out, I was directed to travel on a road heading east. Very little wildlife, other than a few squirrels, a rabbit, and crows, were observed. The carcasses of raccoons and deer were plentiful in the ditch line. The full circle of life from birth to death to feed the living. Just outside my right ear I heard, "You cannot understand the present until you understand the past."

The depth of that truth vibrated in every cell of my body. Tears and a smile became one.

The road bent and twisted, down a hill and back up again. Old buildings tucked in along the valley road caught my eye. I stopped whenever I was pulled into the energy of the buildings. The old buildings are the mirror to life. New, stronger buildings take their place, supporting the families that their ancestors once depended on. Remembering and understanding my past led me here. It has been washed clean. I am born anew. Stronger and wiser, appreciating the past and all its joys and sorrows.

Echoes

Author: Sherry Mikkelson

She runs into the wind
Not knowing where it will carry her
She trusts it knows the way, or she just doesn't care
She only knows that she is driving away from what she
needs to leave behind
Wanting answers but not knowing the question and that
some questions are not meant to be easily answered
On she drives in her quest for enlightenment
To something sacred.
She is the only one visible in the car, but she is not alone
The spirits of time are with her,
some angels too.
Moving forward the car goes as if it had a mind of its own
They will guide it where it needs to go
The air caresses her skin
As beams of sunlight, filled with promise, smile down upon
her face
Her face, that for now, cannot smile.
The light endeavors to penetrate her soul, to eliminate the
feelings of being dismissed

Defeated but determined. Her face a stony stare.
Her angels try to comfort her. They whisper….
'Trust.' 'We will lead you to a sacred place
Surrender and let us guide you.'
The road to epiphany is long, bumpy, sometimes harsh but beautiful.
In the broken we find answers, we find what is real, what is true, what is beautiful
Animals dead in the road as birds circle above. One life is done and others are nourished.
Past fields and trees and pastures. Past rivers and streams. Past old bridges, houses and barns….
'STOP!' the invisible passengers shout
She stops
She looks, she listens, she feels, she hears;
'Calm in chaos, beauty in ugly, transformation. Out of the ashes it rises; we rise.
She is asked now to do what seems impossible
'YOU CAN', she hears as she moves forward
One building is on fire
She is called, compelled to walk through that fire
She trembles. She doesn't want to. She is afraid of what they have to show her.

She fears but knows, with faith, anything is possible and
does what she once thought was impossible.
She walks to it. Through the fire she goes.
She does not burn but she feels the pain and joy of so many
spirits
Of so many memories.
She finds clarity and closure
The fire reveals truths unspoken and a path to peace
Some fires cannot be avoided. They will flare up until they
are attended to.
She emerges, unharmed, out the other side and the building
is whole again.
Broken buildings. In the barns only forgotten straw remains
Dark and hollow houses, what ghosts reside in those used
up places, those rooms that once held life?
Broken buildings, empty rooms, stories to tell, beauty to
share
Not unlike our hearts and souls
Renew memories, create more
Old is never old, it is woven into the new
The past is never gone, only forgotten, it is meant to be
remembered again
It awaits the arrival of the future

Always changing, ever evolving
Worn, ragged and lost, we come to a new understanding
We too, can relate to those broken buildings
Like the Velveteen Rabbit
Once we feel old, worn, ragged and lost, no matter our age
When we have loved and have been loved, when we have cried and smiled, raged and praised…
We become real
We understand
We are beautiful.
'Becoming', is not always easy or fun but always beautiful
She is by herself, but she is not alone
Her angels and spirits of the past are traveling with her.
Desolate houses. Broken windows. Rusty nails and twisted hinges.
Abandoned but not alone. Those spirits are with them too.
They give life to what seems dead.
What stories can they tell?
'Listen!' they say. The voices speak. Silently the shadows creep. They know the secrets.
Whispers in the wind… 'Listen, watch, feel.'
This old barn, this old house has a soul

She stops. She listens. She feels. In her soul mind, she sees and hears.
They watch each other in this sacred space.
She is in the presence of the Divine.
In the fields, among the trees she hears them say; 'Nothing is ever lost
and 'broken' is just a perspective.'
The trees speak; 'the barn is our brother, our father, our mother. We are one.
These buildings were made from our ancestors. We stand, reverent in your presence
and invite you to do the same.
Honor the past, present and future that all meet here.
In this sacred place where children played, fields were plowed, planted and harvested.
In this house where tears were shed and love was made and families prayed. Where meals were joyfully eaten and babies were born.
She could see the clothesline that once held tiny clothes, large overalls and a mother's best Sunday dress, the one with yellow roses.
There is the bridge where Grandpa once sat with his fishing pole

As giggling children, pants rolled up, splashed in the water and scared away the fish

And Grandpa smiled and joined them.

The same bridge that would one day be crossed by the family's children, one by one,

as they grew up and said goodbye as children

and returned with families of their own.

She could hear the happy barking of the dog who lay buried beneath the tree but whose spirit was still alive and well.

From old comes new. Even among the debris, there is beauty.

Nothing lasts forever, not sadness nor happiness, but we evolve. We grow.

We are not separate from the past. Life goes on.

Sometimes beautiful

Sometimes ugly

Sometimes both.

"Look for the beauty in the ugly' one of them said to her, though she could not be sure who

She looked. There on a fallen down beam, she saw it. Her comfort, her peace, her renewal, her epiphany.

In her mind's eye she saw the little caterpillar, about to give up,

so it surrendered.

It crawled inside it's chrysalis and surrendered.

It turned to mush.

She moved closer to the broken beams of the barn and witnessed the emergence of a beautiful butterfly.

She again heard a whisper. 'becoming is sometimes painful and hard, but when you are ready, you will grow wings and fly.

On that long car ride home she smiled. The light had gotten through.

Her car was full. Full of angels and spirits and one very visible butterfly

She had clarity, new perspective and connection.

We are never alone, never really lost.

Seek and you shall find

Beauty is all around you and your answers are always there.

Chapter 19
The Wind Chime

Sunday evening, Marilyn and I sat around her table discussing the current situation with the graduation invite. I then called Gary, letting him know I would be home the following day. While on speaker, the three of us talked about this being about our granddaughter. This is her graduation day. It wasn't her fault this split had occurred. The grandchildren wanted me there. I agreed to go, with an escape route if needed.

The evening of my return, our youngest son came into the house and embraced me. He said he was scared, not knowing where I was. Gary had called the boys, informing them I had left. The beginning of his apology sounded sincere. He then began sharing and questioning me as if I were a child, telling me that an education is to develop an income. Did I have a return on my investment?

"Spoken like a true capitalist," I responded.

His view was that this is a hobby. He insisted that I am wanted at the graduation, as he had spoken directly to his older brother. I wasn't so sure. At the end of the conversation, I made it clear that this fed my soul, and that it was the very thing that saved me mentally and emotionally, versus seeing a therapist for twenty years. I am able to give back to the world in ways others cannot.

Mother's Day arrived as another day in the neighborhood. Gary tells me that our youngest son and family are coming over around dinner time.

"Why? What has changed?"

His facial expression and body language indicated that I was being difficult. My thoughts went to when they were arriving, which was dinner time. Are they expecting a meal? What did I have to feed seven people with dietary needs? How unfair that I am to feed people on short notice, and on Mother's Day. Gary insisted they weren't expecting food. I bought a cheese and cracker tray with an assortment of vegetables just in case. I was feeling uncomfortable and hesitant. He was anticipating something different.

Sure enough, everyone comes bounding in, phones in hand, planting themselves on the living room furniture. I can only imagine that my "antics" were viewed as a childish temper tantrum. I didn't fit into their religious concepts. I am the stranger, the outsider, the rebel, the lost soul. Gary disappeared into the bedroom, our son on his phone, smiling.

"What is going on?" I ask.

All smiles, both of them said nothing. With effort, a seven-foot by two-foot box was laid on the table. The phone is shown to me. I caught my breath because our eldest is on speaker. How do I respond? A huge gift lay in front of me. His wife and children remained sitting in the living room, slightly away and with their backs toward us.

Well, this is uncomfortable, I thought. Taking a breath, I called on my guides for direction, holding onto some sense of decorum. Everyone is so proud of themselves, totally unaware of my discomfort and the reasons for it.

Inside the massive box was the wind chime I had been coveting for several years. Oh, the deep song that it sings when teased by the wind. "This is over the top, but accepted with gratitude," I respond.

The silent question of who engineered all of this was answered. The son who hadn't spoken to me suggested they all chip in to pay for it. It took my running away to give them a moment to consider what their world would look like without me in it. The undeniable truth was this wasn't about me; they made it about themselves. *How dare I scare them.* This was easing their guilt.

Friends who were aware of my need to run away spoke of their concern, fearing I was suicidal. They had never heard the depth of despair in my voice before or seen the action of me driving west with no plan, no concrete destination. I had taken off with only trust for the pilot guides, trusting them completely. Four years ago, I had plans to leave for a week without giving notice and simply drive away. I'm not sure why I didn't. Maybe it wouldn't have made the impact needed. I was screaming inside, a long, mournful, silent scream.

This scream felt like the final long push a mother gives before the baby enters the world. This cleansing scream, after years of releasing anger, is what I believe to be a birth into the new.

Our relationship has taken another leap forward, just as it had several times before when I couldn't deal with the dead or dying energy between us. Gary is a good man. He has done many amazing things for me. What I wanted and needed, he could not provide. To stand up for me when life and people hurled hurtful accusations and lies; to hold me with comforting arms. I needed emotional support. Honoring who I am has been a lifelong process. Needing someone to protect me. Needing to know that protecting me or standing beside me was an action of love. This need reaches back in time, needing protection physically and emotionally from people, especially Mother, looking the other way.

Picking up the breadcrumbs laid down for me to follow, sometimes the size of loaves, I followed. Unlearning the old me and replenishing with the breath of my awakening soul's journey. A huge chunk of impostor syndrome was left back in the hills of Viroqua.

Chapter 20
Seeking Authentic Love

The holidays were fast approaching, and I had another decision to make.

Christmas was my favorite time of year. The spirit of hope and magic filled the airwaves. Classic movies like *Rudolph the Red-Nosed Reindeer*, *Jack Frost*, *Frosty the Snowman*, *Charlie Brown Christmas*, *Babes in Toyland*, *The Little Drummer Boy*, *Miracle on 34th Street*, *The Christmas Story*, *A Christmas Carol*, *White Christmas*, and in my adult years, *The Polar Express* were a few that continued to warm my heart, lending hope for humanity.

In grade school, the Christmas carols we practiced for weeks led up to the Christmas programs marking the holiday break. Art class took over the classroom, making a gift for a parent with Christmas music playing in the background. My soul felt a hopeful, joyful peace.

As an adult, I tried to make Christmas special for my sons, even on a tight shoestring budget. I didn't always succeed, but it wasn't out of lack of trying. Each passing year, I added to the collection of decorations, building a

Santa collection from after-Christmas sales and yard sales. Santa always brought a sprinkle of magic, hope, and unconditional love, even for the naughty boys and girls.

This past year has been riddled with jar-shaking insights within myself and how I was perceived. Clarity began to unfold when I asked for physical and ancestral healing during one of the first shamanic journeys. The message received was: “Seek authentic love.” As the year progressed, deeper, wiser insights trickled in, directing me closer to the answer to what authentic love is.

Running away certainly was a major step in seeking authentic love, by putting distance between myself and the clanging insanity. Done! Done! Done! How many times in my adult life did I say that I was done? Each time, the energy shifted, opening the door for awakening and healing. This time was different. I was becoming more aware of what my triggers were and the why’s.

All the classes taken awakened me to explore the world around me, but more importantly, to explore the depths of me. Tracking and judging what I could have done better, or at the very least, differently. Are these mistakes any different from anyone else’s? No! I gave until there was nothing more to give, but it wasn't enough. Having accepted that I have been judged as a failure, my bones ached with the weight.

With the approaching holiday, it felt like five bands were playing simultaneously in a ballroom in my head. I began automatic writing to clear away the disappointed, cluttered thoughts and emotions. I needed clarity.

My fingers began spelling out "authentic love." My heart fluttered, fingers lifted from the keyboard. *Seek authentic love...stand your ground* rang in my ears. My long-time deceased grandfather and granddaughter Makayla, during a recent journey, had said to stand my ground. Allowing my fingers the freedom to type, I was now piecing together what I had intuitively always known.

Love isn't only an emotion; it's an action word. *Love your neighbors as yourself.* I had allowed those I loved deeply to gaslight me. I had listened to everyone tell me what they thought I needed to hear, and I dug into self-evaluation. No more! I have done my emotional and spiritual work, and now I stand my ground.

I must love myself through love in action. Respecting myself and stopping the insanity is what Makayla and Grandfather spoke of. For my body to heal fully is to recognize and honor the authentic love within myself. My pancreas represents love. To turn this around is not only about food and the medicines my body had rejected; it's about deep emotional healing!

The imprint of my childhood experiences had been traveling with me, interjecting the doubts of not being worthy to succeed and to be loved by others; that I have value and deserve respect. Apologizing for things I had no control over really meant that I was sorry for taking up space.

I listened to others with compassion, giving support as needed and honoring their wins, but who was listening to me? None of my accomplishments were recognized, or if they were, it was halfhearted acknowledgment. Gaslighting was alive and well.

Not feeling important hit the hardest. For years, I have been practicing setting healthy boundaries. Here I stand, knowing this past year was where the rubber met the road, hard and fast.

I deserve better than what has been handed to me. The miracle is that without these individuals, would I have learned this valuable lesson? If it were not for them, no, I wouldn't. I bless them for their presence and their part in my awakening.

Saying you love someone isn't enough. Love involves being present because you *want* to. Going months and years without a word is not love for either one of us. This lifetime is about healing karmic wounds and completing contracts. This is my purpose. Once the contract has been seen for what it represents, I am no longer attached to that relationship. I am free to respect my health through love in action. No more will I knowingly or willingly remain in a situation that is affecting me mentally or emotionally. That energy plays out physically.

I allowed the message "seek authentic love" to simmer, allowing the answer to appear rather than logically forcing it. The image of my mother and mother-in-law standing over the stove tending to the simmering ingredients by watching it closely and waiting for that perfect texture to form before removing it from the heat came to mind. Internally, I knew the message meant a need for generational healing. It had been simmering since before I was born. It has taken me nearly seventy years for the imprint of generational trauma to unravel and be put into action. Healing isn't a sprint but a marathon.

The choices I have made, the boundaries I have adjusted, did allow others to follow or not follow suit. In time, you may be surprised. My running away literally opened into a paradigm shift. Conversations are returning as are healing relationships once believed to be dead. With each action step, change is in the air.

The season's winds play the massive chime in the background. Its deep song reminds me that all is well.

Chapter 21

Authentic Love Isn't Passive

Living your authentic self has been spoken of by nearly everyone who is traveling the spiritual path. Do we really comprehend its deeper concepts? I don't believe so.

Do you know what your core values are? Do you understand what healthy boundaries are? It's imperative to know in order to awaken to your authentic self.

Are you living in fear, frustration, or anger and surviving to make it through another day? Do you have hope and see the light at the end of the tunnel becoming brighter and touchable?

Living your authentic self requires exploration into the shadows of your ego self. It's about being honest and becoming aware of the motives behind your words and actions. Are you appeasing others to keep the peace? Knowing when to speak up or remain silent is an art form. Are you making excuses for others' disrespectful behavior? Have you made amends to those you have intentionally or unintentionally harmed? The internal shadow work holds the golden key to living your authentic self, which develops into an authentic life that transforms into authentic love.

Remember, love is not only an emotion for another but requires action to confirm that love. To love your neighbor as yourself is a respectful action. Loving your neighbor (others) isn't always easy, especially when they can be jerks. You can respect their right to breathe and walk their own journey. Respect without placing judgment because you don't have all the facts. Everyone is in the classroom, some at different grade levels, studying different subjects.

Chapter 22
Why Is This So Important?

Publishers ask what is the goal and reason for publishing a book, and who is the target audience? I knew the why and who for my first two books. With the original book tile, *Following the Breadcrumbs*, the why and who weren't immediately clear. Years ago, I began authoring stories centered around what the animals were mirroring back to me. They and my studies taught me enough to keep me out of the therapist's office and many others if I'm being honest with myself.

Within the pages of my life, people came and went. Some stayed longer, and often, the important players returned. Are there others like me, or am I "special?" Being special is the need to fill a void within. It was something I could relate to in the past, but not now. We are a part of the whole; we are not complete if one part is missing. There has been discussion around which major organ we could live without. Transplants have drastically changed that question. The organs can be kept alive even if the brain is dead. The truth is that our body requires all working parts to function properly, even if we don't fully understand the importance of a spleen's purpose. It is the same with everything in the natural world.

All my experiences within these pages were a working collective of my guides and teachers drawing me ever closer to right here, right now. The "why?" unveiled itself months later. When scientists thought we had junk DNA, it was because they hadn't seen the deeper connection of our DNA strands. They now understand that it has multiple functions such as gene regulation, genetic evolution, and structural support. Will there be more to learn and explore? Oh, I can hardly wait to see the what and the why. We, as new souls and older souls, embrace the concept of being a scientist and learning how our soul develops and how it's connected to every living thing, including the microorganism the naked eye cannot see.

Why is this important? Within my ordinary, extraordinary life, I have awoken to the possibilities beyond my current vision, and so can you! You are the author of your life. You get to choose to get started or stand still; it's always your choice. Many people need rules and structure, like guardrails along high ledges and long, wide curves along the roadway. Structure and guardrails keep us safe. Then there are those who live on the edge, daring and challenging life itself.

When keeping the mind and heart open, answers always appear and opportunities to explore, oftentimes in mystical ways. As I have experienced, the mystical experiences appear before the question has been formed. The answer to "What does this mean?" may take years of unfolding before revealing the purpose. This is faith. One step at a time and trusting unseen forces is what we are called to do.

As a child, I questioned and observed my family and events. It seemed as if I knew on a soul level that this time around, as an incarnated soul, it would be different. Different in the respect that the energy of victimhood would no longer be my frequency. Like the phoenix rising from the ashes, so will I. For this to happen, karmic patterns and debts must be recognized, and responsibility taken for my role. How would I know how to forgive if I didn't have anyone to forgive? How do I learn about relationships if everyone was perfect or pretending that they are? Experiencing difficult times is necessary for growth. We can learn through observation, and yet that too has its drawbacks. We can keep asking, "Why is this happening to me?" without really wanting to know. If you are serious about the why, be ready for the answers, because you may not like what you are facing within yourself. Face it you must if you desire freedom.

Everything is a mirror. You can judge and condemn, but in some form, you were once the very thing you are judging and condemning. Not one of us arrived as an old soul knowing what we know. We started like infants, learning to sit, crawl, walk, and run. This planet is an educational planet, the perfect school *if* you decide to explore, learn, and oftentimes unlearn. Spiritual growth requires each of us to stop blaming others and our past stories. Those stories hold a golden nugget of wisdom to glean from *if* you choose to look with a new pair of eyes.

The Mystical Life Experiences of the Awakening Shaman recounts the mystical experiences pieced together that led out of the imprints of my soul's journey. I accepted that I have value and am worthy to receive by surrendering the falsities once placed upon me and carried silently. Impostor syndrome has been given notice.

I hope you decide to sail your vessel, dance inside the fire, and live authentically full out.

AND I GIVE THANKS FOR ALL THAT WAS, ALL THAT IS, AND ALL THAT WILL BE.

About the Author

Linda Ledbeter is an Intuitive Spiritual Mentor, Animal Whisperer, Author, Speaker, and Shaman. She assists people and animals in navigating their life experiences with compassion. Linda is an ordained Minister and Counselor with All Light Ministries and *A Course in Miracles*. She serves as a Practitioner in Healing Touch for people and animals, Reiki Master, Shaman, Mystic, and Akashic Records reader.

She believes and practices that every aspect of life experience provides a window into self-awareness. Every mystical experience, person, and animal that is or has been in your life has a purpose. Difficulties in the present are linked to past lives. In her writings, this concept is conveyed through personal experiences and personal responsibility. Linda's life purpose has been about giving a helping hand when and where she can; one of her mottoes is to simply show up and be present. The amendment to that motto is: show up and be present for yourself too.

Linda has come to embrace that all of life's experiences are sacred and that everything has a purpose. It is for the individual to explore their shadow side because that is where the golden key is waiting. It is not a sprint; it's a lifetime marathon of discovery.

Linda can be found at:

https://www.facebook.com/linda.ledbeter.14

Website: https://lightwindshealing.com

Email: lightwindshealing@gmail.com

Podcast: ProjectCommunication@ProjectCommunication-WI

Look for further books:

Thriving Beyond Crisis: Conversations With Resilient Entrepreneurs
Chapter 11: "I Asked, I Received, I Screamed"

The Art of UNLEARNING, Vol. 5
Chapter 2: "Intimacy = In To Me I See"

A Foster Dog's Journey: Highlighting Ernie – Reality Meets Reality
Moonbow Publications and Productions LLC, Menomonee Falls, WI

www.ingramcontent.com/pod-product-compliance
Lightning Source LLC
LaVergne TN
LVHW020046110826
845155LV00029B/644

* 9 7 8 1 9 4 9 5 1 3 5 3 0 *